CW01640757

A Pilgrim's Guide to STONEHENGE

A Pilgrim's Guide to STONEHENGE

The Summer Solstice Celebrations
Winter Solstice and Equinox
Dawn Gatherings

Jim Rayner

Copyright © 2012 Jim Rayner

All rights reserved. No part of this publication may be reproduced or transmitted in any form or by any means, electronic or mechanical including photocopying, recording or any information storage or retrieval system, without prior permission in writing from the publisher.

The right of Jim Rayner to be identified as the author of this work has been asserted by him in accordance with the Copyright, Designs and Patents Act 1988

First published in Great Britain in 2012 by
The Choir Press

All illustrations and photographs by Jim Rayner unless otherwise stated

Front cover photograph of the 2009 winter solstice sunset by
Jim Rayner

Cover design and back cover photographs from the 2007 summer solstice celebrations by David Slater

ISBN 978-0-9562190-8-4

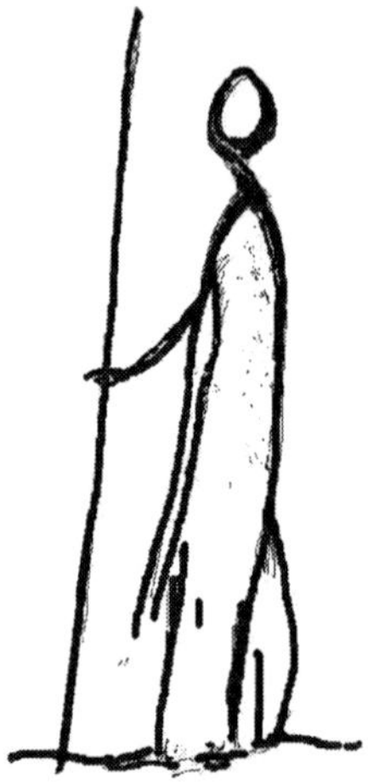

Contents

Acknowledgements

Without the help and encouragement of the following people this book would not have been possible. Particular heartfelt thanks to my wife, Julie, for her copy editing and proof reading skills and to our two children Grace and Felix for supporting me throughout all the site visits and seemingly endless hours on the computer. I would like to thank my mother, Chris, my sister, Helen and my aunt, Linda for their ongoing support and encouragement. This project would also not have been completed without the generous editorial help and regular advice from Helena Hughes. I am also greatly indebted to my brother-in-law David for his much appreciated help with the photography, graphic design and cover design.

Other people to thank include Hugh Newman and the Avalon Rising earth energies group, whose talks gave me the inspiration to start my research; Lokabandhu and all those involved with the Buddhafield Yatra walking meditation to the stones in 2005; my local Community of Interbeing meditation group; The Auriga Mystery School; The Natural Nurturing Network; Fee and Kevin Warner from Mercury Moon; and finally the two Essex University hitch-hikers Shar and James who accompanied me to the stones in 2009.

The aim of this guide

This book has been developed as a guide for those intending to make more of Managed Open Access (MOA) as a meaningful and fulfilling pilgrimage. Its aim is to provide information for anyone wanting to know more about what goes on and how the quality of the experience can be enhanced through ritual and understanding. This has come from my own experience of having attended the celebrations on a number of occasions and feeling the need to know more. I felt there was a clear need for a pilgrim's guide that enabled the modern visitor to become more of a proactive participant. As a result, this book focuses on ideas, suggestions and information about what to expect. Apart from wandering freely amongst the stones, much of the information can also be applied to the normal visiting times throughout the rest of the year. Also included is an overview of the historical context, a proposal to reveal the Altar Stone and an examination of how the summer solstice could potentially be developed in the future.

Chapter One

The growing attraction of the summer solstice

Introduction

Stonehenge is a place of spiritual significance, created by the ancients to mark cycles of life, death and rebirth. It is a memorial to the ancestors, an astronomical calendar, fertility temple and gathering place of many possibilities all rolled into one. Here on the earth is a deceptively simple, yet deeply powerful structure.

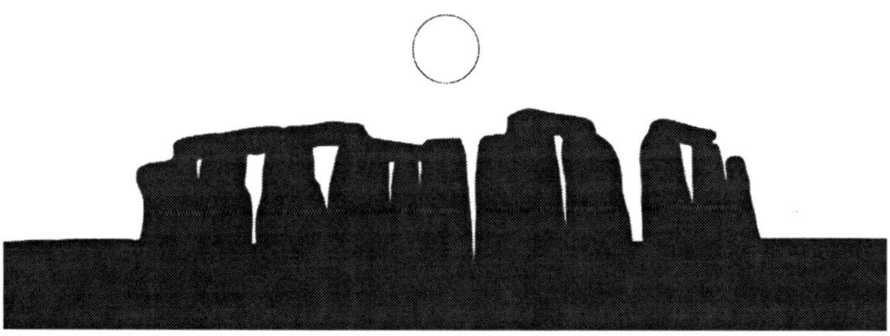

Stonehenge and the Cosmos

Every year nearly a million people visit Stonehenge, with an increasing number coming for the summer solstice celebrations. English Heritage, the public body and custodian of Stonehenge, provides the framework and organisation for people to access the stones at solstice time, but they do not lay on a concert or activities. This was decided during the original discussions leading up to the granting of MOA in the year 2000, whereby 'free and open access for all' was restored. A great deal of what happens during this 'open occasion' is therefore left up to the attendees to decide for themselves.

Sunrise at Stonehenge with winged banner unfolded to greet the sun

The first recorded celebrations

In more recent history, the first sizeable groups to visit the stones, other than passing travellers and nearby townsfolk, were nineteenth-century day trippers often using the railway to Salisbury as a connecting point. At the turn of the twentieth century ownership was transferred from private hands to the nation and modern-day Druids started to hold ceremonies with groups of onlookers. Revellers looking for a place to party were also attracted to the site and numbers began to grow. Over the next few decades crowds ranged from a few hundred, to a few thousand, when the solstice fell on a weekend. Later, by the 1960s, the site became a focus for alternative and countercultural ideas and subsequently, a large annual 'free festival' emerged from 1974 onwards. As a result, Stonehenge became a 'people's temple open to all'. By 1985 however, the festival's associated 'peace convoy' of travellers was ambushed by the police in the infamous 'Battle of the Beanfield' and proceedings came to an end. An antagonistic exclusion zone was then set up around the stones for the next fifteen years.

People, however, still yearned to gather at this special place and the demand for access would not go away. Peace negotiations rumbled on for several years before a high court ruling finally deemed the exclusion zone unworkable. In 2000, English Heritage and Wiltshire Constabulary finally agreed to open up the stones for a few hours of Managed Open Access and the modern summer solstice celebrations came into being. Perhaps the high cost of maintaining the exclusion zone also had something to do with the change of heart. Whatever the exact reasons for re-establishing the right of access, the creation of

MOA (which includes the winter solstice and equinox dawn gatherings) has been a positive step in the right direction for all concerned.

The attraction of the celebrations

So, who actually attends the modern celebrations? The answer is many different groups of people – including members of all the main Pagan groups such as Druids, Wiccans, Witches and people who term themselves 'Pagan' in the widest possible sense. A good number of tourists, locals, hippies, students, bikers, travellers and goths attend, along with many curious onlookers and people out to party. A few historians, spiritualists and astronomers come along, as do some adherents to eastern religions such as Hare Krishna devotees and practitioners of Buddhist meditation and yoga. Amongst the crowd, the odd celebrity has even been spotted every now and again. The celebrations also prove to be a big draw to people from abroad. MOA has become a wide-ranging occasion open to anyone who wants to come, gone are the days of exclusion.

At the start of MOA, the middle of Stonehenge is soon filled with revellers cheering to an undulating beat of drums. The majority of the crowd however, sit and stand around the outside edge of the stones waiting for the sun to arrive under the ambient glow of retractable floodlights. A simple sheet of rules, known as the 'Terms and Conditions of Entry' is provided to all attendees but, apart from the time of sunrise and the preceding sunset, there is a distinct lack of information about other events. Yet, even with this lack of knowledge about things to do, the celebrations are a major draw. The lack of any structure is there to allow the occasion to develop from the ground up, rather than be imposed from the top down.

Ready to start, the crowd at the beginning of the 2007 summer solstice
Photograph by David Slater

General view of the 2006 summer solstice celebrations

The nature of celebration is to have a joyous time and it is interesting to note that the United Kingdom has amongst the least number of public holidays in Europe. People work increasingly long hours and the stresses of fast-paced living can take a toll on the body, as well as the mind. The longest day of light is a natural place to focus attention and take a break from the normal routines of everyday life. Stonehenge fulfils its role as a communal gathering place, because it can be so easily identified in the minds of so many people.

The solstice represents a free space where ideas can germinate. It is a place where people can follow in the footsteps of the ancients, party all night and mark out an alternative path for the future. Without the vision of the original festival goers, and the campaign for access after the Battle of the Beanfield, little of this would have happened. This process included all those who kept turning up at the stones and attempted to celebrate the solstice, throughout all the years of exclusion.

The legacy of the festival is still a contentious issue for those who argue for the right to gather for a few days. English Heritage, local residents, the police and National Trust, who are the major landowners around the site, all continue to express their concern that the original free festival had become unsustainable. In their view, it had grown out of all proportion to the site and threatened the archaeological landscape. They believe the same would happen if another free festival emerged and that the best way forward is through the structure of MOA. In some ways, the current summer solstice celebration does contain one core element of the old festival in being free at the point of entry. Apart from that, some would still argue that it is a very different event.

Many modern revellers still attend the summer celebrations hoping to find a 'rock festival' with bands and DJs taking centre stage, whereas today, they actually get a 'festival with rocks'! This can result in a number of people wandering around not being quite sure what to do with themselves in the absence of amplified music. The decision not to allow amplified music was taken in the build-up to the creation of MOA. It was felt that the required infrastructure, generators and staged music would take longer to organise and cost considerably more. High decibel levels were also deemed as being inappropriate to the spiritual experience.

The Glastonbury and the more recent Sunrise Celebration festivals however, often start directly after the solstice. When this happens Stonehenge is effectively used as a staging post with many travelling onto Somerset afterwards. In 2006 when the Sunrise Celebration concluded just before the solstice, many chose to stay on at the festival site rather than travel onto Stonehenge. A fully fledged music festival is therefore an attraction in its own right with or without the focus of seasonal change. Andy Worthington notes this distinction in *Stonehenge Celebration and Subversion*: 'Even during the free festival years, the number of people actually visiting the stones on the solstice was rarely more than a few thousand. As the festival grew, the spiritual significance of the temple dwindled, so that two thirds of those attending the festival in 1977 visited the stones at solstice, but only a thousand out of the 40,000 did so in 1984.'[1]

Panoramic view of the 2007 summer solstice
Photograph by David Slater

When the solstice falls on a weekend it is another factor to take into consideration. Friday and Saturday night solstices are generally much more popular than ones held during the week. The appeal of the occasion therefore does have its limitations, especially when factors such as the weather, other festivals nearby, and even international football matches involving England are taken into consideration. The FIFA World Cup and the UEFA European Championship finals begin in June and key matches can coincide with the celebrations.

Summer solstice sunset 2007
Photograph by David Slater

The night time party

Revelry is a key feature of the solstice and many attend with the aim of getting high. For most, having a drink at the solstice is no more than a social lubricant but, unfortunately, for a small minority the use of drink and drugs can take on a slightly anti-social element with misplaced exuberance around others. This can be especially difficult for those with young children.

Catching some sleep in amongst the summer solstice party debris

Whilst drunkenness will always be a feature of the summer solstice, the antisocial aspect to the revelry can often be quite shocking for those expecting a more sedate occasion. The celebrations can certainly enthral an audience, but they can also disappoint. The lack of respect for the site created by the debris of the all-night party scene has led some people to ask themselves the question – would they really want to go again? The very nature of Stonehenge is that it is all things to all people and thankfully most attendees do treat the site with respect and take a positive view of the place. A small band of volunteer 'Peace Stewards' are on hand to give general advice and help defuse tensions with the unruly few.

In reality drunkenness at the stones only mirrors drinking culture in wider society. Plenty of people are out to seek a party at Stonehenge, in much the same way as weekend revellers do in any British town or city centre. The Druid Arthur Pendragon in a paper prepared for the Association of Sacred Landscapes states that: 'A sacred site should give off the aura of inclusivity, rather than of exclusivity'.[2] This suggests that the excessively drunk should be incorporated into the occasion rather than being shut out altogether.

There is also a growing opinion amongst archaeologists and historians that psychoactive substances were used at ancient solstice celebrations, through the use of naturally available fungi, plant extracts and dried herbs. This would have been a way of communing with nature and contacting spirits in shamanic-type rituals. In the book *Hengeworld* Mike Pitts notes that: 'It is not a joke: some of them, it seems, really were stoned.'[3] Perhaps the emphasis on excessive hedonism is a continuing part of an ancient tradition and a ritual for some in its own right. Funded by the Arts and Humanities Research Council (AHRC) 'The Riverside Project' was a major archaeological study of the wider Stonehenge landscape which ran from 2003 to 2008. When Professor Mike Parker Pearson of Sheffield University and his team excavated Durrington Walls, Stonehenge's original supporting settlement, they found a substantial number of small animal bones linked to seasonal feasting. These finds suggested that in the distant past, Stonehenge was a place where people went to party, albeit with reference to the winter solstice, rather than the summer one.

Bringing matters back to the present, public safety is paramount in the minds of the authorities, and memories of the football crowd disasters of the 1980s, combined with the current climate for 'compensation culture' has led to a cautious approach. Local authorities and governmental agencies generally like to organise their own events, rather than subsequently manage ones which have grown out of the public imagination. The solstice at Stonehenge is exactly this type of situation and MOA could be described as a negotiated compromise between a wide range of interested parties. Anyone who has followed the story of solstice access over the last few years will have no doubt realised that excluding people just does not work. Stonehenge is a temple open to everyone and the saying 'bring what you expect to find' is probably the best piece of advice for anyone attending the celebrations.

Gathering crowds by the Heel Stone
2009 summer solstice

Chapter 2

Contemporary Paganism and self-directed rituals

Stonehenge is part of the British countercultural 'season' and the solstice gathering functions as a focal point for popular imagination. The celebration also draws worldwide media attention to one of the most visible gatherings of Pagans, Druids and others interested in nature-based spirituality. Whilst Stonehenge was not built by the original Iron Age Druids, it is certainly associated with modern ones today.

Interest in nature-based spirituality has certainly grown in the last few years, not only in the British Isles, but further afield, particularly in North America, Australasia and continental Europe. The term 'Pagan' is taken from the Latin word 'Paganus' meaning 'country dweller' and was given to those rural locations still practising the 'old ways', often with reference to worshipping nature and natural cycles. Today, the word 'Pagan' is really an umbrella term encompassing a wide range of beliefs. It is unlike monotheistic religions in that it does not have one all powerful godhead figure, messenger and centralised text. It is polytheistic and to some extent pantheistic (polytheistic: having many gods and goddesses, pantheistic: tolerating different forms of worship) and embraces many traditions. Interest in Paganism is on the increase and people can either join a group or follow a more individual path. There is a whole host of supporting information for people to examine. In the book *Pagan Pathways* the following list[4] was compiled to sum up three generally shared tenets of Pagan belief:

Kinship with Nature
Concept of a Goddess and God
The Pagan Ethic: Do as you will, but harm none

The question, however, is what do Pagans and Druids actually do? Often any ceremony is perceived by the general public as being esoteric and not easily understood. Mainstream reviews of the summer solstice only refer to ceremonies in generalised terms, without actually explaining what they are about and what actually goes on.

In Paganism the circle is an expression of the sacred
Here a circle is combined with a 'Triskelion' or three-pronged interlocking symbol

A Pagan ceremony usually begins with people coming together to form a circle. This creates a sacred space within which all stand equal. At the quarter points, the elements of Earth in the North, Air in the East, Fire in the South and Water in the West will be bid welcome. Special readings will then take place with blessings, calls of divinity, chanting and songs. Other ritual acts can include the spreading of seeds into the circle's centre, the handing out of ribbons, the lighting of candles and the movement of the participants around each other in an intertwining fashion. Food and drink can also be shared. Finally, the directional spirits are thanked as the circle is unmade and the ceremony ends.

Druid and Pagan ceremonies at Stonehenge

In all its detail, a large and formal Druid ceremony can take well over an hour to complete. Because of this several of the modern-day Druid Orders perform their ceremonies outside of MOA. They can then gather in peace and remove any possibility of being interrupted by an overbearing crowd. This explains why some people are mystified as to why they do not see more Druids at the summer solstice. A greater range of Druids however, can be seen at the winter solstice.

Modern Druidry is a Pagan religion and stems from the antiquarian and romantic movements of the eighteenth, nineteenth and twentieth centuries. Little is actually known about the original Iron Age Druids. Modern Druids are organised into numerous groupings or orders and, whilst there is much common ground, there are also many differences in style and interpretation. Other differences can exist between Druids, Wiccans and other Pagan groups in terms of belief and ritual practice. All Wiccans are Witches, but not all Witches are Wiccans for example. Almost all groups, however, usually stand in a circle and call elemental corners as a basis for ritual.

One of the most visible groups of Druids during the actual summer solstice celebrations is Arthur Pendragon's 'Loyal Arthurian Warband' (LAW) Druids. They perform a short ceremony in the centre of the circle at sunset and another by the Heel Stone at sunrise, with any interested bystanders. The participatory aspect of these ceremonies is based around the principle of call and response. Amongst acknowledging the four elemental directions and a call for peace, the Druid Vow[5] and I-A-O chant are recited.

The Druid Vow and I-A-O chant

'We swear by peace and love to stand, heart to heart and hand in hand Mark, O Spirit, and hear us now, confirming this our sacred vow.'

The **I-A-O** chant is a western mantra similar to the eastern ohm. It is chanted in one long breath and a different tone for each letter. This happens as follows: 'I-I-I-I-I-A-A-A-A-A-O-O-O-O-O'. The 'I' represents the phallus of the solar god, the 'A' the mother earth goddess and the 'O' the passage of the earth around the sun. Sometimes, the Druid call of **Awen** (pronounced 'Ah-wen') is also chanted three times in succession.

The three-pronged Druid 'Awen' symbol representing rays of light from the Sun. Also included in this illustration is a new, half and full moon

The summer ceremony symbolises the transfer of power between the Oak King who reigns when the sun grows in strength or waxes and the Holly King who rules when the sun wanes. This is the contradiction, that although the sun is at its most powerful at midsummer, it will now start to wane before its rebirth at the winter solstice. During the winter solstice and both the equinoxes this publicly accessible ceremony is usually performed in the centre of the circle.

Self-directed rituals

Performing rituals can be a powerful activity, linking a sense of self with that of place and community. The Pagan writer Walter

Wright Arthen notes that: 'Repeated ritual provides a kind of language which allows for the communication of subtle meanings across generations, even when those transmitting the message do not understand it. Our problem, as we recreate our tradition is to rediscover the patterns of old rituals and make them contemporary.'[6] This is a key point as regards Stonehenge, as patterns of ritual can be made contemporary. The past is respected, but there is a clear view about taking things forward. The path to being a Pagan is almost whatever you want it to be and this can stem from initiatory Druid orders and Wiccan covens, to more open groups and individual paths. Although Paganism was described by Cole Moreton in a *Guardian* newspaper article as: 'a rainbow of revived, recreated and reinvented beliefs.'[7] this need not matter. It is a case of examining how comparable rituals and folklore traditions can fit with Stonehenge here in the modern age. The act of being able to perform your own self-directed rituals could be the way forward for Stonehenge, as they provide the opportunity for first-hand experiential understanding without having to join a group or take intoxicants.

Whilst some people do perform rituals during the celebrations, many do not. The overall aim of this section is to examine what sort of ritual acts can be undertaken by those who have an interest, as in order to succeed they have got to be well tested, easily understood and have relevance to the occasion. Whatever you do at Stonehenge it will have to be done in amongst or around what currently goes on. A group of friends, a family, a couple or any number of individuals may want to perform a small ceremony at Stonehenge involving a few rituals. Whether this is any combination of standing in a circle, chanting or acknowledging the four directions, it serves, in the words of Glennie Kindred and Lu Garner, the authors of *Creating Ceremony*, to: '... bring people together and unite them in common purpose.'[8] When rituals are repeated time and time again they can gain in power and create a shared sense of continuity. Performing rituals at sacred sites can potentially influence the planet's health as our thoughts, words and deeds can influence what happens in physical reality. Whilst many Pagan rituals are directed towards worshipping nature, their effect on people must not be underestimated. In his book *Needles of Stone*, Tom Graves says of this: 'The energies that rituals create are not in themselves physical, but they are made real in a physical sense by the way in which they affect people's attitudes, and thus their actions.'[9] Stonehenge can be a place of mixed emotions and the aim here is to utilise accessible rituals in order to take the vibrations to a more positive and inclusive level.

The Kumbh Mela

Across the world, mass gatherings and large-scale pilgrimages can be undertaken with a greater sense of personal involvement. Known for its vast size, the Kumbh Mela in India is just one of these events. A major gathering happens at the confluence of the Ganges and Yamuna rivers every twelve years, according to planetary alignments and movements of the sun and moon. What happens during the Mela could be described as a kind of chaotic carnival, mixed with peace and spirituality. There is much that can be learnt from this event and how it relates to solstice at Stonehenge. In the case of the Kumbh Mela, the practical action involves everyone taking to the waters for a symbolic dip with processions of the various Hindu sects and holy men (sadhus) adding to the occasion. The organisers provide a simple instruction for those taking to the waters often just before dawn: 'Take a cupful of water in your palms and sprinkle it in all four directions while reciting prayers.'[10] Performing such a ritual can add a greater sense of personal involvement in the whole experience.

A bewildering dawn

Back at Stonehenge, apart from the party in the middle of the circle, the main shared experience is based around watching the sunrise. Whilst this can be very dramatic on a clear day and even raise a collective cheer from the crowd, generally early morning mist and cloud cover can often make the sun invisible. In such conditions, the actual moment of sunrise can often bewilder an audience, especially as the dawn sky starts to lighten well before the sun's appearance over the horizon. People stand facing the right way, at the right time, but there is no sun to be seen until the sky clears. The whole thing can then end up becoming a bit of a damp squib with many people leaving early. Instead of one dramatic moment of light bursting over the horizon, the process of sunrise can actually be a rather protracted happening. After witnessing one rather grey Stonehenge dawn, Steve Lowe and Alan McArthur, the authors of *Blighty – The Quest for Britishness*, describe their experience: 'After waiting up all night, did we see a majestic dawn with rays of golden sun light showering down upon us? No was the answer. The scene before us actually comprised of lots of people standing around waiting for a cloudy sky to get brighter.'[11]

Simple rituals, however, can add more to the experience because they are things you can do for yourself regardless of the weather. At least a few other people will be doing something similar throughout the course of the celebration, so you will not be alone. Rituals therefore provide a platform for personal empowerment and form a basis for connecting with nature and its seasonal turning points.

Street Ritual

If you intend to perform a ritual at Stonehenge some people may want to watch what you are doing, ask questions and even join in. Generally this is not a problem, but some spectators may want to interrupt, especially if you are in a large group. This is why many Druid Orders opt for their own access times where they can be left alone.

Starhawk, the Pagan writer and environmental activist, offers some good advice about performing rituals within the midst of 'energetic environments' such as protest marches, festivals, camps and other gatherings. To work in such environments, she has developed a fast style of moving ceremony called 'Street Ritual'. Here she explains that: 'Street Ritual requires a somewhat different set of guidelines to the normal rituals we do under the full moon, in the woods or even in the protected, enclosed and safe urban space. Here are some basic guidelines, keep it simple, simple and simple.'[12] The reward of being able to perform any number of simple rituals through the distractions of the summer solstice can be worthwhile. Starhawk goes on to say that the reward of 'Street Ritual' is: 'dynamic, exciting and ever changing.'[13] By focusing on simple things you can do for yourself, the practical application of 'Street Ritual' can be seen to work and provide a greater sense of meaning to your pilgrimage. At Stonehenge, the aim is not to feel too conspicuous, but conscious about why performing rituals can be important.

Saying hello and offering a blessing

The issue of how people interact with ancient sacred sites is an interesting question. Most people generally like stone circles and other places of antiquarian interest, but what is the best way to seek meaning from such places? Some people like to look and wander, for example, without feeling the need for any further exploration, whilst others like to perform ritual or make merriment. It all comes down to subjective interpretation and personal responses.

A good start to this process of investigation comes from Giles Bryant who makes the following points about approaching stone circles and other places of antiquarian interest: 'Firstly introduce yourself to the site you are visiting. All sites have particular energy, and waltzing in without being welcomed is rude and disrespectful. Many dowsers have noted that stone circles often have a guardian or entrance stone which can react to people's energy. Literally turning on, or shutting down energies in reaction to the thoughts and intentions of those about to enter.' Bryant goes on to summarise by saying: 'We all have different ways of doing things, but saying hello is generally a good idea.'[14] Another note on visiting ancient sites comes from the *Northern Antiquarian* website. Here it states: 'Your ability to feel the subtle nature of an ancient site is wholly dependent by the way which you enter the place.'[15]

Generally held to mean 'the light in me recognises the light in you', 'Namaskar' or 'Namaste' is a simple gesture undertaken with the palms together before the face or heart whilst bowing. In India and Nepal this is used as a greeting and such a blessing could be used to open your time at Stonehenge.

Sprinkling water or seeds and saying words to the effect of 'I give thanks for spirit around' can also help set the tone of your visit. In Japan, before entering a Zen temple or garden, pilgrims can often sprinkle water on the path or ground before them. A rock cut bowl and ladle are usually provided for this purpose. Sprinkling water functions as a purification ritual and the supporting chant of 'Ware Tada Shiru Taru' focuses on personal responsibility. This Zen saying could be interpreted as, 'If you learn to be content you are rich in spirit.'[16] By doing this, participants can focus on fertility, blessing the land and acknowledging the spirit of place. If you want to use seeds or herbs which are not readily available you might have to think more creatively about how to get hold of them. I have ended up buying some St John's Wort teabags from a health food store, getting a seasoning jar of thyme from a supermarket and ordering some chippings of oak bark online, although I did manage to get some holly from a local bush! I sprinkled the oak bark to symbolise the coming of the Oak King at midwinter and used the St John's Wort, thyme and holly at midsummer.

Sprinkling water as a blessing at Kit's Coty Dolmen in Kent
Photographs by Julie Robins

Making a wish can also be done in conjunction with leaving offerings. There is some debate, however, about what could be termed 'ritual litter' when tea lights, tinsel, dream catchers, wrapped flowers and even personal items are left at various sites. Whilst some sites do have specific traditions associated with them, it is worth thinking about how what is left behind may be perceived by others.

Sprinkling 'Water in the West' as part of the Buddhafield 2005 Yatra which concluded at the Stonehenge summer solstice celebrations

Circumambulation
The ritual act of walking all the way around

The *Buddhamind* website describes circumambulation as: 'making a clear and conscious connection with something that is regarded as special. The nice thing about circumambulation', it states, '... is that it is incredibly simple – anyone can do it, even those with small children.'[17]

In Wiccan terminology, a clockwise movement is referred to as 'Deosil' and is used to invoke, create and open. The anticlockwise direction is known as 'Widdershins' and is associated with closure and release. What is interesting here is that English Heritage direct visitors around Stonehenge in an anticlockwise direction, rather than encouraging the idea of traversing the temple in a symbolic clockwise direction. However this may change in the future when new visitor guide books and audio tours of the site are published.

The importance of the clockwise movement, therefore, should not be underestimated. It is the act of following in the footsteps of the ancients and mirroring the movement of the sun which would be the point of the exercise. Whatever the ancients did at Stonehenge, they could well have walked around the outer edge of the circle. John Toland, one of the founders of modern Druidism, noted a Scottish oral tradition of ancient people having circumambulated cairns, wells and standing stones: 'according to the course of the sun'.[18] A surviving example of just such a ritual can be found at Struell Wells in Northern Ireland. Here, several clockwise circuits of the well heads can still be undertaken in order to earn 'merit' and provide a focus for a visit. Struell Wells once had its own raucous summer solstice celebrations based around these rituals. There are many other examples of ancient sites having various traditions of 'going three times around'. These include the dolmens of Kit's Coty in Kent, Arthur's Stone (Maen Cetty) on the Gower Peninsula and St Lythan's Chambered Tomb also in south Wales. The basic theme of walking around is similar to that of Buddhist pilgrims circumambulating a stupa or reliquary. Stupas have some similarities to Neolithic tombs in being constructed as special places to house the bones, ashes and other relics of the dead. Over time practically all chambered tombs have lost their contents and become ruined. To visit such places today we are making a connection with the symbolic nature of these ancient structures. By circumambulating we are acknowledging the passage of our own souls and consciousness through time. These places have been there for a long time, but our own physical journey might be more ephemeral.

Walking around or circumambulating a sacred site has many practical benefits. It is a good way to mark the fact you have arrived and to acknowledge the place as being special. The author is seen here with his young son walking around Kit's Coty dolmen in 2009

Photographs by Julie Robins

To emphasise the movement of the sun, the outer stones of Stonehenge are numbered one to thirty starting in a clockwise direction, from opposite the incoming Avenue and Heel Stone. A modern Druid ceremony can start with a 'sunwise' walk into or around Stonehenge and conclude with an anticlockwise movement flowing back out from the centre. Whilst Stonehenge is often seen as a place with no specific purpose or defined use, circumambulation is the sort of simple and tangible act that can be seen to work. Acknowledging the course of the sun is an identifiable ritual and an extension of what people are already doing. It is also worth noting that if someone were to film visitors walking around the stones over the course of a normal day and then played the film back at speed, the resulting visual swirl would look very dramatic.

In the book *Pilgrimage*, Simon Coleman and John Elsner state that the act of walking all the way around a temple or shrine: 'ritually defines the sacred space and marks the fact that the pilgrim has arrived'.[19] Walking around the stones can therefore carry great meaning. Please note that this can take longer during the summer solstice celebrations. The main entrance, food stalls, toilets and gathering area are all located around the western edge of the stones where it can be very crowded. To complete your circumambulation you will probably have to take a wider line around the stones at this point. At the winter solstice and the equinoxes a simple lap of the outer edge of the circle can take as little as two to three minutes. Please note that the Heel Stone can also be used as a focal point for circumambulation and marking the elements.

Buddhafield Yatra circumambulation of Stonehenge in 2005
Photograph by Steve Smyth c/o Mercury Moon

Marking the elements and four directional quarters

Marking the elements and four directional quarters is an essential component of ritual. Each element sustains and counteracts the other providing, along with spirit, the building blocks of life. Keeping things simple, the elements can easily be marked by reciting the following flowing rhyme by Andras Corban Arthen: 'Air I am, Fire I am, Water and Earth and Spirit I am.'[20] This could be done on the way round as a constant mantra, in one spot or in each of the four directional corners depending on how you feel.

Greeting the dawn and calling the Element of 'Earth in the North'
Loyal Arthurian Warband solstice ceremony Stonehenge 2006

Yoga

Acknowledging the light and warmth of the sun is one of the main reasons many come to Stonehenge. The great fiery orb sustains us in every respect, for without it we cannot grow and evolve. The yogi Dr Svami Purna states in *Yoga: A Practical Introduction* that: 'Constantly without discrimination, this powerful dispenser of life energy sheds its rays on everything alike, remaining equally unaffected by splendour or squalor. Each human being is a microcosm of this gigantic energy system.'[21]

As long as you have some understanding of the postures (asanas), then performing some basic yoga moves at Stonehenge can be a positive experience. Probably the best location for yoga is on the incoming Avenue where there is plenty of room. Practising at sunset or sunrise provides the practitioner with two auspicious times, but yoga can equally be performed at any time of day. Aim to keep your awareness not solely on the physical exertion or movement but the whole experience.

The yogic 'Salutation to the Sun' (Surya Namaskar) is a set of twelve individual moves which join together to form one flowing asana. Usually one to twelve rounds can be performed, but on special occasions, such as the solstices and equinoxes, a special number can be undertaken by very experienced practitioners. This is usually done as a charity fundraiser or a personal challenge. Known as a 'Mala', this consists of 108 salutations and is usually undertaken in nine blocks of twelve rounds to the accompanying rhythm of a drum or a guiding mantra. The number 108 has many connotations, as the renowned yoga teacher Shiva Rea explains: 'The average distance of both the sun and the moon to the earth is 108 times their respective diameters. There are 108 Upanishads (Hindu scriptures), 108 'marma' points or sacred places of the body and traditionally prayer beads have 108 beads upon a string.'[22] Whilst performing 108 rounds is probably too much for the average person, undertaking at least one salutation or a few other postures would still be a good way to acknowledge the high point of the solar year.

Yoga: 'The Triangle Pose' at Castlerigg Stone Circle, Cumbria and 'Downward Dog' at Silbury Hill in Wiltshire

One noticeable yoga event which takes place at sunrise during the celebrations is the 'Yang Spiral' meditation organised by the Tara Yoga Centre. Here a pre-arranged grouping of alternating male and female participants stand holding hands in zodiac order beginning with Aries. The pattern is then repeated for as many times as there are people. Several hundred people have been known to make up such a spiral elsewhere. This synchronised meditation works well at Stonehenge for it taps into the unfolding power of the universe. Participants report a subtle flow of energy and wellbeing when all standing together in this way. Interestingly the spiral unfolds in an anticlockwise direction to release the build-up of energy back out into the world.

Acknowledging the sun to conclude

At the time of sunrise Druids can 'hail the sun' by raising a hand or a wooden staff into the air whilst other people can raise a toast and 'thank the sun for giving life'. To further expand this concept of venerating the sun, a channelled Native American spirit called White Eagle adds another perspective by saying that: 'Ancient wisdom teaches that behind and within the physical sun is the spiritual sun or white light. The ancients were taught how to use this white light for the blessing of life on earth.'[23] To conclude your time at the stones you could simply stand in quiet reflection, cheer a clear sky or perform a yoga sun salutation asana.

Watching the summer solstice sunrise at the Twelve Apostles stone circle, Ilkley Moor, West Yorkshire, 2010

Chapter 3

The winter solstice and equinox dawn gatherings

The other times of Managed Open Access

English Heritage also grants Managed Open Access for dawn gatherings at the winter solstice and spring (vernal) and autumn equinoxes. The winter solstice gathering generally takes place on either the 21st or the 22nd of December depending upon when the astronomical date of the solstice falls. This also applies to the equinoxes which fall between the 20th and 22nd of March and the 21st to 23rd of September respectively. Please note that the summer solstice celebrations are held on an established date of the night of the 20th and morning of the 21st of June. This happens, irrespective of any variation as to when the actual astronomical timing of the solstice may fall.

The other times of MOA, however, go with the flow and fall on the right date in question. The one exception to this rule is when the astronomical timing of the winter solstice or both the equinoxes falls after sundown. Access is then on the next day to coincide with the birth of the new sun. So the exact timing of the winter solstice in 2009, for example, fell at 17:47 hours, just over an hour and three quarters after sunset. Access was therefore on the 22nd, even though the actual solstice was on the 21st! English Heritage, however, has been known to allow a short period of unofficial access (running from about 07:30 to around 08:30) for those who turn up on the 21st. However, please do not rely on this always happening.

Due to these reasons, I would strongly advise that you check the official date of access before attending, as things can be somewhat confusing. To further complicate matters, English Heritage tends not to advertise these other periods of MOA online. Access dates and times can, however, be found elsewhere on the web and you can always ring or email the English Heritage office in Salisbury nearer the time to confirm. One other additional note would be to take into account the weather and if the date of access coincides with a weekend. A bright and clear winter solstice or equinox dawn gathering is likely to be much busier if held on a weekend, than in comparison to one held on a wet midweek morning. Although having said that, weekend gatherings tend to be more accessible and a larger crowd can make for a more interesting event.

The winter solstice marks the turning of the year with Stonehenge receiving around eight hours of daylight. At midsummer however, daylight can extend to some sixteen and a half hours. The opening time for winter solstice MOA takes place between the hours of 07:30 and 09:00 (with sunrise just after 08:00). At the equinoxes, access runs from approximately 05:45 to 08:00 at spring (sunrise at around 06:10) and 06:30 to 08:00 at autumn (sunrise at around 07:00). Please note that these times can vary and English Heritage reserves the right of access until it is deemed light enough to enter the stones. Entry is free to the stones for the winter solstice and both the equinoxes. A more peaceful atmosphere often prevails at these other occasions, firstly because they are not so well known and, secondly, because the weather is often much colder!

Winter solstice MOA dawn gathering 2005

The growing appeal of the winter solstice

In 2005, a record number of people (1,500) turned up at the dawn of winter, an amazing fact considering only a few years earlier numbers had barely reached a few hundred. The winter solstice is also a better time to see people interacting with the site in a more contemplative way. I have witnessed participants playing crystal singing bowls, bells, gongs and tuning forks, and notes of peace being left along with people meditating, practising yoga and walking around the stones.

'Circle of Sound', winter solstice crystal singing bowl ceremony in 2005

A tuning fork held aloft in the middle of the stones in 2005

Right: people meditating with a small Buddha statue in 2006

Whilst the midwinter sunrise is now becoming an established event, the preceding and much fabled midwinter sunset is still only observed by a small number of people. The celebration of the winter solstice sunset, however, could well have been the real occasion in ancient times, as Christopher Chippindale notes in *Stonehenge Complete:* 'On midsummer solstice day, 25,000 or more people now go there in the middle of the night to see the sunrise in exact astronomical alignment – but on the wrong day; they should really go in a December afternoon to see the midwinter sunset'.[24] As the sun sets just after 16:00 hours on the shortest day, the timing falls within English Heritage's normal opening hours, so anyone wanting to park and visit the stones would have to pay the usual charges. It is possible to stand back down on the Avenue, but the view of the sunset is more distant and is not as immediately accessible.

A clear sunset coinciding with the winter solstice is rare, but it can happen. One was recorded in 2004 and amazingly in 2009 there were a number of crystal clear skies around solstice time. As the sun stops moving at this time of year the symmetrical sunset can occur on a number of days either side of the solstice. I attended on the 20th of December 2009 – after realising that the weather would be clear I hastily booked the day off work and drove down just in time to catch the sunset. I took my place by the Heel Stone and witnessed the truly amazing sight of the sun setting right into the heart of the monument. There was just enough room for the group of about twenty or so other people present for everyone to get a decent view. I took the following photographs of the 'sun burst' which lasted for about ten minutes before the great orb slipped below the horizon.

Left: the symmetrical midwinter sunset: Right: people watching

The final moments of the sunset

The idea of redefining the current winter solstice MOA to include time for the sunset is a wide-ranging issue. The circle, for example, may well have to be lit and various health and safety concerns addressed. During the winter months public access is denied after dark, so extending access beyond nightfall would be difficult.

Winter solstice dawn embrace from 2006

Chapter 4

Visiting guide

General information

Apart from being able to wander freely amongst the stones, much of the visitor information presented in this section could easily be applied throughout the rest of the year. During the normal hours of opening, the stones are cordoned off behind roped barriers and are strictly off-limits. Seasonal opening times apply and the stones close earlier in winter and later in summer. Check the English Heritage website at www.english-heritage.org.uk for further details and current admission prices. Private times of access can also be arranged with English Heritage.

The summer solstice celebrations

If you are arriving via public transport then the Wilts and Dorset bus company run a special all-night bus service from Salisbury train station to the celebrations. Please refer to the www.wdbus.co.uk website for the corresponding timetable. The drop-off and pick-up point for this special solstice bus service is located on the A303 which is about 1.6 kilometres (1 mile) to the east of the stones. The walking route from here is by the side of the A303 and is clearly marked.

If you are arriving by car then follow the signs to the designated parking area next to the new visitor centre. Depending on where you park, the stones can be up to 2.4 kilometres (1½ miles) away via an official walking route running parallel to the old A344 road.

Summer solstice generalised running order 20th / 21st June	
*19:00**	*Solstice car park opens and start of public access to Stonehenge*
20:00 onwards	*Suggested walks in the surrounding landscape. Time for self-directed rituals and to explore the stones using the 'Things to do and find' map*
*21:00**	*Druid ceremony inside or around the main circle*
*21:25**	*Sunset*
*22:15**	*End of dusk twilight*
*04:00**	*Beginning of dawn light. Time for self-directed rituals and to explore the stones in the build up to sunrise*
*04:00**	*First bus back to Salisbury*
*04:30**	*Druid ceremony by the Heel Stone*
*04.50**	*Sunrise*
*06:00**	*Last admission to the car park*
*08:00**	*End of public access to the stones*
*12:00**	*Solstice car park closes*
**Approximate timings and disclaimer: Please note that the celebrations are subject to official confirmation each year and the details and times are subject to change. The author therefore accepts no legal liability for any disappointment or loss caused through any intended use of this list*	

A gathering area is provided for acoustic musical performances and look out for other things taking place around the stones. In previous years English Heritage has also provided two brazier fires as extra gathering points.

English Heritage reserves the right to refuse admission and close the site without prior notice. A full list of summer solstice 'Terms and Conditions of Entry' can be found on the English Heritage website.[25]

English Heritage's Terms and Conditions of Entry:

Alcohol: Only small amounts of alcohol for personal use will be permitted

Animals:	Dogs, pets and other creatures are not permitted in Stonehenge, except registered assistance dogs
Bags:	Only small bags or rucksacks (similar size to hand luggage on airlines) will be permitted into Stonehenge
Drugs:	Illegal drugs are still illegal at Stonehenge as they are anywhere else. The police will be on site during the access period and will take immediate action against anyone breaking the law
Fire:	The nature of this access makes any real flames extremely dangerous. Please do not bring or light fires, flaming torches, candles or fireworks
Glass:	As some people walk barefoot and livestock graze in the area glass items may not be brought into Stonehenge
Lighting:	In the interests of public safety there will be ambient lighting throughout the night. Lights will be systematically dimmed as dawn approaches
No Camping:	Camping is not permitted at Stonehenge or in the solstice car park or anywhere in the surrounding National Trust land
Respect:	Stonehenge is seen by many as a sacred site - please respect it and each other. Drunken, disorderly or antisocial behaviour will not be tolerated
The Stones:	In the interests of personal safety and protecting the special site, please do not climb on the stones
Under 16s:	Children under the age of 16 must be accompanied by an adult

These conditions also apply to the winter solstice and equinox dawn gatherings. Your bags may well be checked upon entry and security staff and other officials will keep watch on proceedings once inside the monument field. If staying all night or just attending a dawn gathering please wrap up warm as it can get cold. As well as the above, it would be advisable to take a knapsack containing some snacks, water and a small umbrella.

Astronomical timing of the summer solstice and relevant moon phase

The exact astronomical timing of the summer solstice is when the sun reaches its highest midday point north of the equator. This same timing relates to the winter solstice in the southern hemisphere. Each year, the timing varies slightly due to the wobble of the earth's orbit around the sun. It is also worth finding out which moon phase coincides with the night of the celebrations. A corresponding full or new moon, for example, can add extra visual and spiritual intensity to the whole occasion. Please see the summer solstice table of access in the appendix section at the end of this book for more details.

Planning a family visit

Before nightfall would be a good time for a family visit to Stonehenge for the summer solstice celebrations. I would also recommend booking into a local hotel or bed and breakfast if you are travelling long distance. Whilst this is not the all-night vigil favoured by many, it would provide enough time to see the stones in the remaining light of day. You will still get a flavour of the event as the party crowd begins to congregate. Another reason for only staying a few hours is that, outside of the main circle and gathering areas, there can be long periods of inactivity and it can get cold. This is not always suitable for young children wanting a warm place to sleep. The walk to and from the solstice car park can also seem like a long way in the middle of the night. It is always advisable to check the weather forecast before your visit. If there is a chance of a clear sunrise then it is worth staying on later. Another option would be to arrive in the middle of the night and have the sunrise as the main focal point of your visit. The other times of MOA are all based around dawn access, so a family visit would correspond with the scheduled times. Whatever period of MOA you choose to attend I would suggest two very short walks in the Stonehenge landscape as detailed below.

Walk One – The Cursus burial mounds

Upon arrival at Stonehenge there is a bridleway or farm access track which runs just to the west of the stones. Walk a few metres down the track until you get to a gate on the left marked 'Stonehenge Down', then walk over to the Cursus burial mounds straight in front of you. This is where the free festival was held in its latter years and the short (500 metre) walk will take you along the route of the festival's main thoroughfare. Although now difficult to determine, the Cursus is a mysterious landscape enclosure, the exact purpose of which is unknown. The name Cursus comes from the Latin name for racetrack, as it was thought that it might have had something to do with parades and processions in ancient times. However, the burial mounds can still be clearly seen and are worth visiting.

Walking over to the Cursus Burial Mounds

Walk Two – The Avenue

Following the A344 road closure, you will be able to walk directly over to the upper end of Stonehenge's original incoming processional Avenue and explore the area down from the Heel Stone. Until then you will have to walk around the edge of the old visitor centre car park. The Avenue offers the best view of Stonehenge and is a good place for yoga and ritual.

Self-Directed Ritual Guide*

Walk over to the top of the original incoming Avenue
which lies a few metres down from the Heel Stone
Then as an opening blessing, stand facing the stones
and say to yourself 'I give thanks for spirit around'
If you have a bottle of water to hand, sprinkle
some to the land

To follow the course of the sun:
Walk around the main circle
in a clockwise direction
(Circumambulation)

Mark the elements on your way
round the circle by saying:
'Air I am, Fire I am,
Water and Earth
and Spirit I am'

Touch the Heel Stone with the:
Open palms of your hands

Cheer the sunrise, if the weather is clear

In addition to the above, face
the sun and conclude with a
'Salutation to the Sun'
Yoga asana

**Please note these rituals can be performed relatively quickly and the list represents a general guide that can be interpreted in your own way. The first few rituals can be undertaken all year round, the last three however, are more specific to Managed Open Access and knowledge of yoga. Words to 'Air I am' ... courtesy of Andras Corban Arthen*

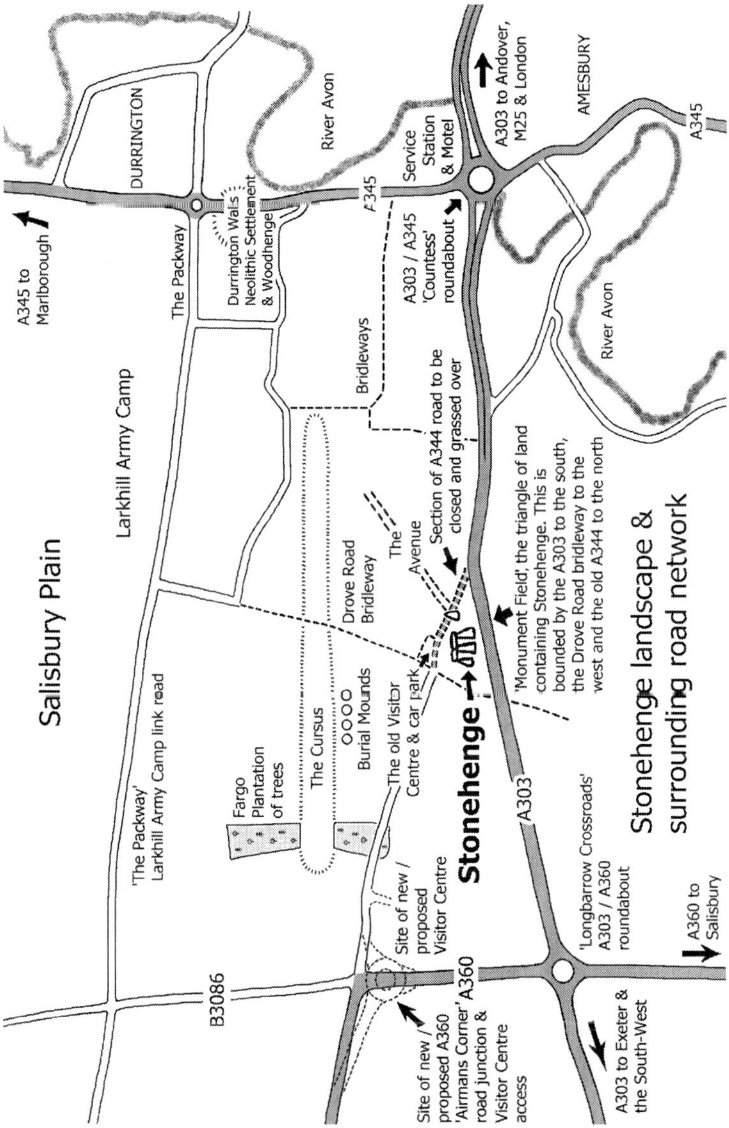
Salisbury Plain
Larkhill Army Camp
A345 to Marlborough
DURRINGTON
The Packway
Durrington Walls Neolithic Settlement & Woodhenge
River Avon
A345
Service Station & Motel
A303 to Andover, M25 & London
AMESBURY
A345
A303 / A345 'Countess' roundabout
Bridleways
River Avon
Section of A344 road to be closed and grassed over
The Avenue
Drove Road Bridleway
'Monument Field', the triangle of land containing Stonehenge. This is bounded by the A303 to the south, the Drove Road bridleway to the west and the old A344 to the north
Stonehenge landscape & surrounding road network
'The Packway' Larkhill Army Camp link road
Fargo Plantation of trees
The Cursus
Burial Mounds
The old Visitor Centre & car park
Stonehenge
A303
'Longbarrow Crossroads' A303 / A360 roundabout
A360 to Salisbury
Site of new / proposed Visitor Centre
B3086
A360
Site of new / proposed A360 'Airmans Corner' road junction & Visitor Centre access
A303 to Exeter & the South-West

STONEHENGE 'Things to find amongst the stones'

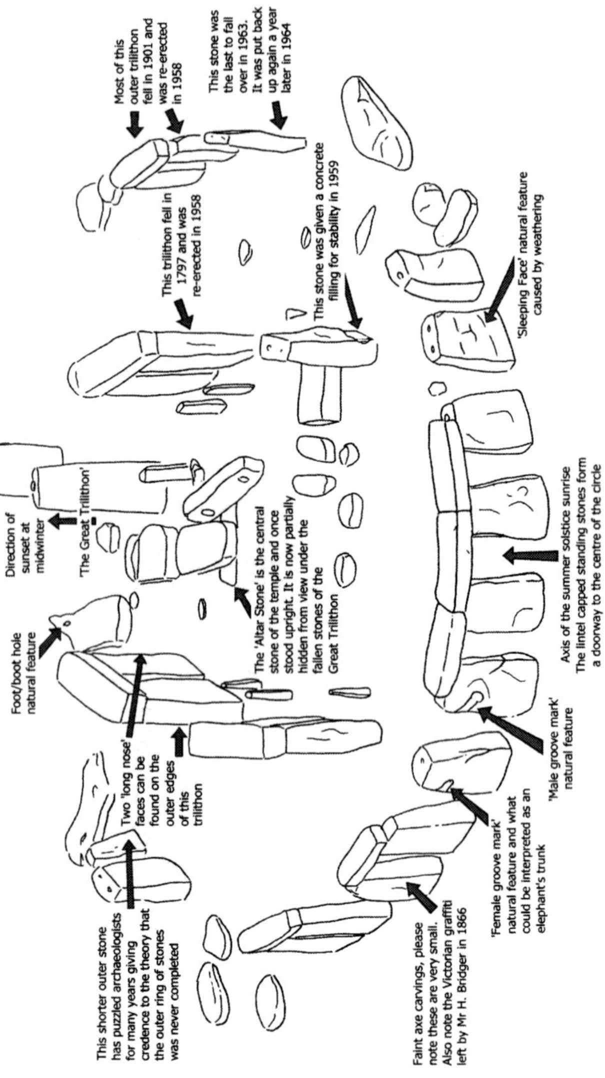

Chapter 5

Sacred stones

Stones as a focus for sacredness

Managed Open Access is one of the few times where those seeking a spiritual connection with the stones can actually interact with them at close quarters. During normal opening hours they are held behind rope barriers and are off-limits to the general paying public. The veneration or use of stones as a focal point for community is an ancient tradition with many worldwide references. Size is not important, as can be evidenced by the tiny meteoric Black Stone of Mecca or the gigantic Mount Uluru (Ayers Rock) in Australia. Sacred stones can represent continuity and outlast many successive generations. They can also arouse great passions and intense feelings. The most contentious place on earth is possibly the 'Dome of the Rock' in Jerusalem. Here the current shrine is based around a section of natural bedrock whose ownership is highly contested between Judaism, Islam and Christianity.

Over a period of several hundred years many of Britain's ancient sacred stones came under sustained attack from religious zealots. The Obelisk, the monumental central stone of Avebury, was toppled over by a puritanical mob in the 1600s and finally broken up sometime after 1724, when the antiquarian William Stukeley last visited the site. Even when it lay flat on the ground the stone would have continued to attract veneration from non-Christianised country folk or Pagans. This could well have involved people touching the stone as a blessing to its ancient presence. Destroying the stone was meant to eradicate these old practices, but some magic must still remain, as people continue to gather in the place where it once stood.

We could touch any rock at any time, but would this be the

same? Maybe or maybe not, as this would be a personal choice and depend upon the rock, location and historical context. The stones of Stonehenge certainly fit the bill of being special, because so much mystery surrounds them. How were they transported to the site and how did the ancients construct such a precise monument, are the usual questions. Other questions would be what have they witnessed over the years and what secrets do they hold? During MOA any of the stones can be touched, the bluestones or any of the major sarsen uprights, but why is the Heel Stone seen as being one of the most potent blessing stones?

The Heel Stone

The Heel Stone is a prominent free-standing monolith which faces the main body of Stonehenge. Its great bulk and size attract attention. It also stands at the end of the incoming Avenue which is where the ancients themselves would have stood when they arrived for the original ceremonies. Symbolically touching its surface with the open palm of your hand is a tangible experience and is something anyone can do. It is eminently possible that the rock could absorb the 'energy' of those who have come before and anyone doing the same today could continue such a process. The pilgrim's progress would then be linked to the past, present and future in one pan-generational action. How many people have come before and who will come in the future? The rock was placed there before our written records began and it could potentially outlast the structures of our present society today. Romans, Saxons, Normans and numerous visitors from other times have all passed this way, and yet the stone has remained. It is interesting to note that when the Romans arrived in Britain, the Heel Stone had already been in situ for well over two thousand years.

Whilst the Heel Stone originally had an encircling ditch, the outline of which can still be seen, and possibly even a partner stone nearby, ancient pilgrims would have gathered in its presence to mark their arrival at the temple. Today, during MOA, people continue to instinctively do the same. The Heel Stone has a number of clear blessing points on its surface, and even though the original custodians abandoned the site some 3,500 years ago, people would have still continued to visit the site. The circle's reputation for healing was well known in the twelfth century when Geoffrey of Monmouth visited the site. This continued right up until early Victorian times when according to Gary Varner in *The Folklore and Magic of Sacred Stone*: 'The stones were still occasionally washed and the water used in baths as a spa-like cure for ailments.'[26] The Heel Stone is usually thought of as being the marker for the summer sunrise, when in all possibility, it could be the 'heal' or 'healing stone' as well. When attending the celebrations, the author has certainly heard people referring to it in such terms.

People touching the Heel Stone at the 2005 winter solstice

Feel the vibes; without any prompting people can be seen approaching the Heel Stone during any of the times of MOA. The top two photographs were taken in 2007 by David Slater and the bottom left in 2005 and bottom right in 2006 by Jim Rayner

Touch is a basic instinct and within that moment you connect with the spirits and mark yourself as a person who has come to this special place. The unifying role of sacred stones could have a positive benefit for our increasingly individualistic and fragmented society. The ancient stones may be talking to us again, but the question is, are we talking to them? The author has stood by the Heel Stone many times during MOA and observed people coming to touch the same places on its surface time and time again.

I have seen a smudge stick ritual, water blessings, notes of peace and offerings of greenery left within its 'mouth'. I have also seen musical instruments played in its presence and a fire juggler who climbed to the top and breathed out a long flame. I once even met a man who said there is a 'guardian' or 'spirit of place' residing within the stone. These are some of the reasons why the Heel Stone could be seen as having such potency. It is interesting to note just how little has been written about the 'spiritual aspect' of the Heel Stone and how it relates to the rest of the Stonehenge experience. The dowsing community, however, are one group of people who do venture into the quirkier side of stone circle research.

Didgeridoo at the Heel Stone

Dowsing energies

Tom Graves explains how someone might go about accessing the 'special energies' of a standing stone: He says: 'Place palms flat on the surface of the stone then at this point; lean against the stone, resting your weight on your palms, and relax. By relax, I don't mean go floppy: rather, I mean that you should allow the tension of your muscles to ease evenly.'[27] The result of this experience would be to literally tune into the vibes and enjoy a quiet moment of contemplation. This is exactly what people are doing during MOA. It just seems to be a natural thing to do. Other dowsers have also identified chakra or energy points within large monoliths and mapped out spirals and flowing patterns around them.

The Bluestones

Another notable stone in the central area is the tall and slender bluestone with its long groove and inwards lean. This is a very beautiful stone with its rounded curves and guardian-like presence. It is probably the most noticeable of all the bluestones and can equally be touched.

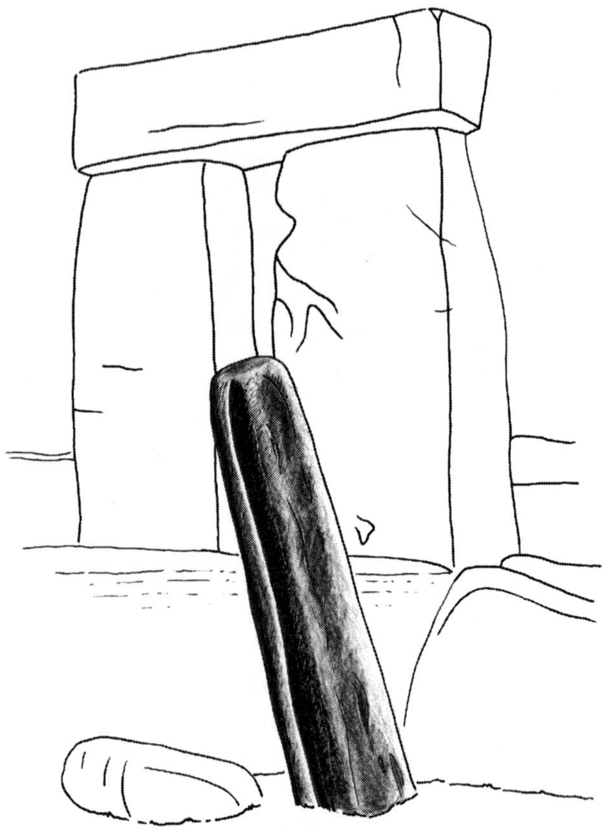

The tall and slender Bluestone (stone 68) with its long groove and inwards lean

The Station Stones

Today, only two stones survive out of an original set of four. The author Terence Meaden refers to the best preserved of these by saying: 'Enough remains of stone 91 to explain its choice, a deep groove along much of its length ... Specialists in mother earth religions, American Indians, Hindus, Tantrics and others, recognise this as a typical female stone, if not a female deity stone.'[28]

The Station Stone (stone no. 91) can provide a good alternative to the Altar Stone for anyone wanting to bless a noticeable feminine stone. Note its long groove and rounded shape

Contemporary theories

Whilst Stonehenge will always retain a sense of mystery, there are many contemporary theories about why it was built and how it was used. Bringing together some of these ideas with what actually happens during the modern celebrations, a picture of what the place is about can start to emerge.

The Avenue approach and the Heel Stone

In ancient times pilgrims would have arrived at Stonehenge via the specially created processional Avenue running up from the River Avon. En route to the stones, the Avenue was carefully planned to dip down into a small valley taking the temple out of view. As the pilgrims then continued onwards and upwards, the great circle would then rise up in front of them in spectacular fashion. Although most of the Avenue is now forgotten, the outline of this last section remains and the effect of reaching the place of pilgrimage via this route is no less dramatic today.

The first major stone you come across is the Heel Stone which is the outlying monolith and summer solstice sunrise marker.

Lines in the grass mark the remaining visible outline of the Avenue on the final approach to Stonehenge. Here the line of the midsummer sunrise and the midwinter sunset diametrically face each other

From this angle you can see how walking around the stones in a symbolic sun or clockwise direction could easily have had relevance to the ancients. Note the bulbous blessing node on the left-hand side of the Heel Stone, as seen in the above pictures taken at the 2006 Autumn Equinox

Touching the 'blessing node' of the Heel Stone right at the start of the 2007 summer solstice celebrations. Photograph by David Slater

Mating of Father Sky with Mother Earth

Interestingly, the subjective representation of a porpoise-like face can be interpreted on the side of the Heel Stone facing the main body of Stonehenge. This phallic shaped monolith is a fertility symbol and is seen to have 'male' characteristics. The Heel Stone had a part to play in the sexual aspect of the circle's design by casting a long shadow right into the heart of the monument. This shadow extended to touch the lower half of the Altar Stone on or around the days of midsummer and represented a symbolic mating of Father Sky and Mother Earth to the gathered onlookers.

The Altar Stone

One of the other principal stones was the single monolith situated right in the heart of the circle. Now known as the Altar Stone, it currently lies flat in the ground and is broken into two pieces. Unfortunately, the view of the stone is obscured by other fallen stones lying on top of it. Archaeological excavation, however, has since confirmed that this central stone did

The Heel Stone is an unworked monolith and was put into position by the builders with its natural face looking towards the main circle

originally stand upright and was placed in such a way that it caught the first rays of light at the dawn of midsummer. The stone was specially selected from the tidal inlets upstream of modern Milford Haven and was obviously brought to Stonehenge for a specific purpose. The composition of this sandstone block is light brown and green in colour and is naturally embedded with mica crystals. Quartz mica crystals can glisten and 'respond' to the stimulus of light.

It is possible that one of the original rituals now lost to us could have involved washing and oiling the stone in order to make the rock's crystalline structure sparkle with special effect.

Seeing the central upright glisten at dawn could have had a profound effect on ancient Britons trying to understand the deeper meanings of life, death and rebirth.

Although the Altar Stone is now a sad reflection of its former self, this special 'female' stone can still reward you with an earthly sparkle when sprinkled with water. Female stones are said to reflect the curves, grooves and rounded shapes of the female form. All traditions have to start somewhere and blessing the Altar Stone is as much a test of faith as anything, due to its position hidden away among the summer solstice revellers.

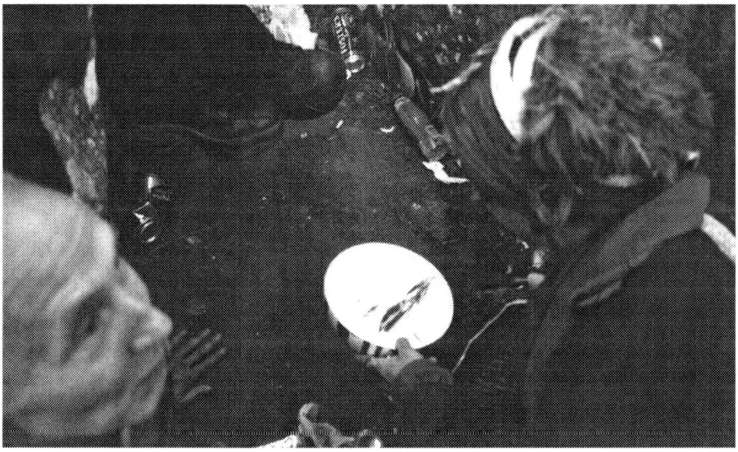

Preparing to bless the Altar Stone with a sprinkling of water during the 2005 summer solstice celebrations at Stonehenge

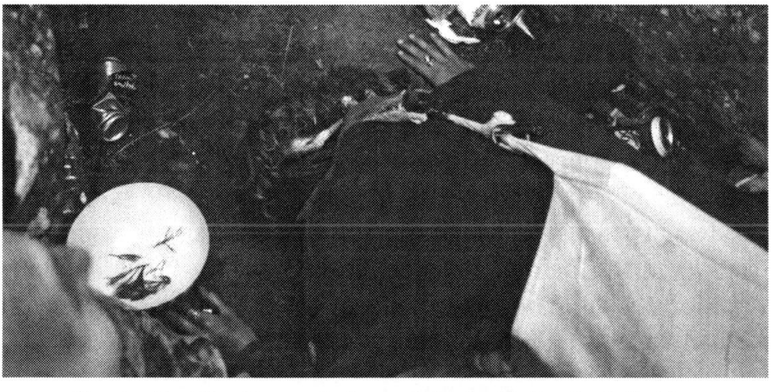

Blessing the Altar Stone out of respect for the Mother Earth Goddess. Please note the surrounding party debris

A better time to interact with the Altar Stone would be at the winter solstice, when the circle is much less crowded. Druids can be seen to bless the stone out of respect for the ancestors and cycles of life.

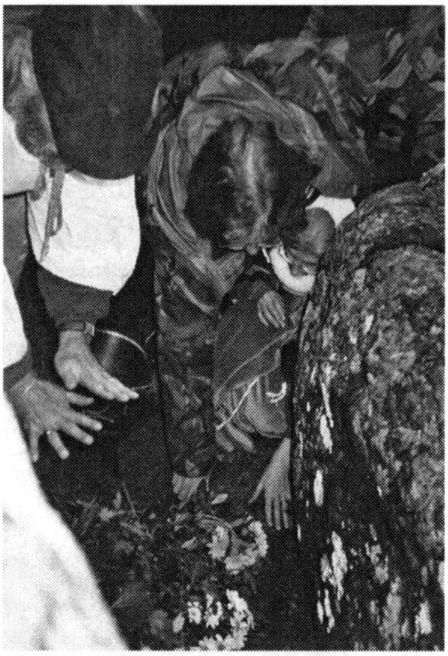

Druids blessing the Altar Stone at the 2005 winter solstice. Note the small cauldron and garlands of greenery

In *Stonehenge – The Secret of the Solstice*, Terence Meaden refers to the Altar Stone as the 'Womb Stone of the Goddess'[29] and gives it prime importance within the temple complex. Placing a 'receptive' stone in the middle of the circle must have been in some ways linked to channel-ling energies between different dimensions, literally trying to see into the nature of time. Perhaps this is not as fanciful as it might sound as quartz crystal can used for healing and channelling. Quantum physicists also match concepts of time with the speed of travelling light.

'The Vagina Monoliths'

The retired gynaecologist Anthony Perks developed a similar set of ideas to the ones noted here. In a 2003 Royal Society of Medicine Journal article entitled 'The Vagina Monoliths' he claimed that Stonehenge was designed to represent a vaginal opening. To support his claim he linked anatomical drawings with plans of the stones. Like Meaden, Anthony Perks supports the fertility theory in which the Sun God comes into union with Mother Earth. The outlying Heel Stone faces the circle in a very phallic way and the main body of stones do include several sexual marks which would help support the fertility theory.

The Stonehenge Altar Stone seen here in its original upright position housed in the centre of the circle

Male and female groove marks in the outer stones

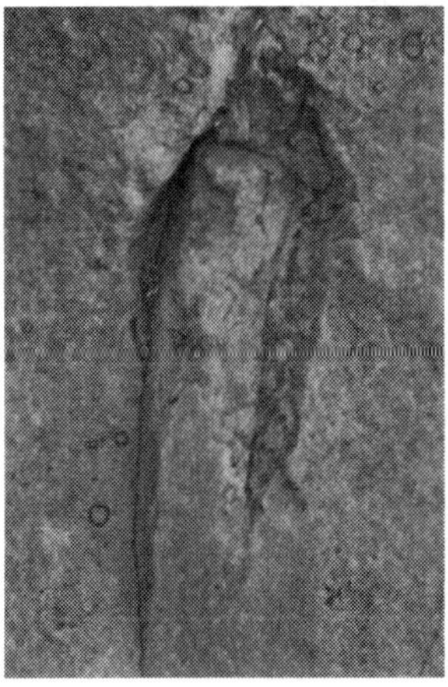

Another mark in the stones representing sexual union

Construction and use

The first interaction with the site occurred some 9,000 years ago with the erection of wooden posts in the vicinity of the old visitors' centre car park. The main three phases of construction using stone took place between 3,000 BCE (Before the Common Era) to about 1,500 BCE. This period also included many sub-phases. The Welsh bluestones arrived on site before the larger, more locally sourced, sarsen stones from the Marlborough Downs. The completed Stonehenge, however, only enjoyed a relatively short heyday of a few hundred years before falling out of regular use.

Much of the current thinking about the circle actually points to the winter rather than summer solstice as being the more meaningful to the ancients. At midwinter, the sun moves along the horizon and sets symmetrically right into the heart of the monument. Acting as a marker, this would have held great significance for a prehistoric people dependent on natural cycles, as the dark of winter would have held great fear of the light and warmth of the sun not coming back.

At midwinter, the sun sets right into the heart of the monument. I have also depicted how the 'moon box' of the Great Trilithon would look if the structure was still standing

The temple also marked the movement of the moon. At the mid points of the moon's 18.6 year cycle, a full moon could be seen setting in the 'higher box' of the Great Trilithon when framed by the configuration of the outer circle (please see illustration). This was best viewed when standing by the Heel

Stone. These astronomical alignments still relate to this central axis today, even though many stones have fallen. To witness these 'sky shows' was one of the main reasons prehistoric visitors came to Stonehenge.

The Ancestors

Professor Mike Parker Pearson believes Stonehenge was essentially created as a memorial to the ancestors. In the early development of the Neolithic religion, worshipping the ancestors provided a primary link between this life and the next. Parker Pearson takes some of his findings from studying native African cultures that still practise this form of religion. When in Madagascar he started to formulate this view, which was then confirmed: 'when a colleague of mine paid a return visit to Stonehenge, took one look at the place and said it was blindingly obvious what it was for – that it was built for the ancestors'.[30] This would explain why we sometimes refer to Stonehenge as a monument, as well as a temple.

Faces in the stones

A number of faces can be interpreted amongst the surfaces, clefts and nodes of the stones and perhaps these were deliberately included to represent the ancestors. Whilst interpretation is subjective, Terence Meaden has noted several examples and Parker Pearson is convinced the rocks are literally memorials to the ancient spirits of the dead.

A weathered sleeping face

Subjective interpretation – can you spot the face on the right with its long nose? The eye of this face is also said to be a female groove mark, as noted previously. Photographs by David Slater

Cremation pits and funerary rites

Around the edge of the ditch there are a number of cremation pits which are known as the Aubrey Holes (they are named the Aubrey Holes after the seventeenth-century antiquarian John Aubrey who first discovered them). There is some debate as to whether these holes (which originally contained wooden posts) were used to calculate solar eclipses, before being later reused to house cremated remains. However, we can assume that in the distant past ancestral spirits as well as the living power of the sun and moon, were celebrated at Stonehenge. Patterns of light and shade and the framing of the sun and moon between the uprights was no doubt part of the plan. This would have been a real crowd-pleasing spectacle in ancient times. But, as with anything to do with Britain, this would have been weather dependent.

Changing weather patterns and abandonment

Changing weather patterns could have contributed to Stonehenge being abandoned, possibly in an unfinished state, in about 1,500 BCE. This date also correlates with early Bronze Age settlements on higher ground being left to ruin as people moved to a more developed system of farming on lower, more fertile ground.

In its prime, Stonehenge was certainly a major centre of power and influence, but over time, ancient Britons would have started to appreciate the rhythms of the solar year for themselves without the use of Stonehenge as a major clock. A hierarchical priesthood that excluded many of the ancient pilgrims in the process of ritual probably did not help either. A range of differing meanings as to what the place was all about must have also led to confusion. Whilst concepts of time some 3,500 years ago were probably much slower than they are today, not being able to see the promised sun and moon shows on a regular basis would have rendered Stonehenge a folly and, later, an enigmatic ruin.

To substantiate this point, Keith Cooper, a professional photographer, watched a clear midwinter sunset in 1976, the year of an exceptionally hot summer. One man approached him from the small group of fellow attendees to say that it was the first time it had been clear since 1964.[31] This modern account serves to demonstrate just how long someone might have to wait in order to see this, the temple's most profound moment.

The weather certainly got Gerald Hawkins down. Hawkins' *Stonehenge Decoded* was noteworthy for his use of an early 1960s computer to calculate astronomical alignments in relation to the stones. He says in the final chapter: 'The worst foe of all was the weather; fierce storms would have been less infuriating than weak mist and gentle rain. Once more I find myself admiring the Stone Age builders – and hoping, for their astronomers' sakes, that the weather then, was not what it is now.'[32]

Obscured sunrise and people subsequently leaving early in 2007
Photographs by David Slater

Sunrise

Anyone wanting to witness an unobscured sunrise might have to wait around for several days, if not longer, for the sky to clear. The ancients would have watched many sunrises, sunsets and cyclic patterns of the moon. Considered observation would have led to the placing of initially wooden posts and then standing stones into the ground to mark various alignments of the sun and moon. The quality of the sunrise would also have been important because different atmospheric conditions can light up the sky in a variety of ways. Sometimes horizontal lines of golden light and even a refracted ray of green light can be seen just above the great orb at either sunrise or sunset.

Earth energies

Stonehenge's relationship with the cosmos and the surrounding landscape would also have been of prime importance to its original designers, not only in terms of how astronomical sightlines correlate, but also how the circle relates to other sacred sites. Some stone circles can be a part of a wider chain, consisting of such things as distinctive hills, springs, wells, rocky outcrops, barrows and other stone circles. Today, these are linked with earth energy or ley lines, following the work of researchers, such as Alfred Watkins, John Michell and Hamish Miller. One of the best-known examples are the fabled St Michael and St Mary alignments. They stretch across the full width of England connecting such places as Glastonbury Tor and Avebury with the rising line of the May Day or Beltane sun.

Although not connected with the St Michael and St Mary alignments, two other major leys have been identified at Stonehenge. One of these links with Salisbury Cathedral and Old Sarum and the other with Glastonbury Tor. Dowsers have found various smaller lines which curve, flow and interact with the site in a multitude of different ways. Part of the original thinking behind the creation of Stonehenge would have involved linking existing flows of energy with the major alignments of the sun and moon. Today, this is known as astro-archaeology and the

Glastonbury Tor

creation of modern stone circles still involves a lot of careful consideration in this respect. In Stonehenge's case is likely that the combination of earth energy and astronomical alignment was aimed at enhancing the circle's 'sacred space'.

Conclusion

Since the creation of Managed Open Access a new audience is being drawn to Stonehenge and new ways of interacting with the temple are being sought. We will perhaps never know the exact nature of the ancient rituals and ceremonies, but archaeologists and researchers can provide a great deal of evidence. Piecing this together, a general picture as to why Stonehenge was created and what it means can be provided. There are many other theories than the ones mentioned here. These include the temple having a wooden roof, two upright 'altar' stones and the inner horseshoe of trilithons being used to resonate sound. The only conclusion is that there is not one answer to the riddle of Stonehenge, but several answers which make up a larger picture of understanding. New interpretations and discoveries are seemingly made every year and our continuing interaction with the place is a valuable activity.

Chapter 6

Revealing the Altar Stone

The current situation

Whilst Stonehenge will always be a ruin, this does not mean further structural changes cannot be made to the layout of the temple. In this section I present a proposal to reveal the Altar Stone and open up the central area of Stonehenge. I feel the time has come for a more open debate on this subject as such a change would vastly improve people's experience of being at the stones, especially during MOA.

The Great Trilithon

A trilithon consists of two uprights topped with a lintel and forms the classic megalithic structure so associated with Stonehenge. The Great Trilithon stood at the head of Stonehenge's inner horseshoe of stones. Only one stone of the Great Trilithon is still standing and this is known as stone no. 56. This stone has a distinctive peg on the top that would have clearly connected it to the fallen lintel below. Stone 56 is the tallest stone still standing on site, at 7.3 metres, and was the first stone to receive the helping hand of modern restoration in 1901, by being returned to an upright position. It had been leaning at a perilous angle for many years beforehand and was likely to fall.

Stone 55, the fallen partner of stone 56, lies broken on the ground in two large pieces. The lower part of this stone is numbered 55a and has a distinctive bulbous base that clearly acted as its foundation. The upper half of the pillar is numbered 55b. Finally, the Great Trilithon's crowning lintel, stone 156, lies in one piece next to broken sections of stone 55. All this then rests on top of the other part of the Altar Stone. The view of the

Left: Stonehenge's tallest stone (stone 56), the surviving pillar of the Great Trilithon
Right: A Stonehenge Trilithon which consists of two uprights topped with a lintel

The fallen pillar (Stone 55a) of the Great Trilithon and its bulbous base

The visible section of the Altar Stone, with the weight of the Great Trilithon's broken pillar and lintel resting on top

Altar Stone is therefore badly obscured with only a small 1.5 metre gap at its widest visible point between the 'v-shaped' formation of the fallen stones.

The Great Trilithon is also located towards the most ruinous part of Stonehenge, which lies on its south-western side facing the prevailing wind. Over the centuries souvenir hunters, vandals, and others in search of building stone have done the rest of the damage.

The Great Trilithon was one of the tallest megalithic structures in the whole of Britain and, because all its pieces survive, restoration might be possible. Stone 55 though, is badly weathered and its two pieces would need pinning back together. I also doubt whether the two halves have enough length to hold the weight of the lintel with any degree of stability without the insertion of a supporting aid and firm foundation. Many of the stones that were re-erected in the twentieth century were placed in concrete sockets. The use of concrete, however, could possibly disturb any subtle energy flows in and around the site, so to do the same today could be problematic.

The generally held view of 'no more restoration' does nothing to rectify the current position of the fallen stones cluttering up the central area. Suggesting that some stones be moved raises many issues with preservationists coming up against those who view Stonehenge as a living temple. Change, however, is part of the natural rhythm and flow of life and in my opinion the current position of the fallen lintel and pillar in the central area is unacceptable.

So, would it be possible to re-erect the Altar Stone?

An archaeological investigation of the Altar Stone was carried out by Professor Richard Atkinson of Oxford University and his team during restoration and excavation programmes in the late 1950s. In his ensuing book, simply titled *Stonehenge*, he refers to whether the Altar Stone had ever stood upright: 'Enough remained to suggest that in its original form it had been squared off at right-angles to the length of the stone with the best preserved end being dressed to a bevelled point, very much like the bases of some of the neighbouring sarsens.'[33]

Knowing that in all probability the Altar Stone did indeed stand upright, Ross Nichols, a Druid from the Order of Bards, Ovates and Druids (OBOD), is of the opinion that: 'The fallen central stone could be released and put upright again. The public would then be able to clearly see what this great temple was and how the rays work in winter, as well as in summer.'[34]

Herein lies one of the answers to improving the visitor experience during MOA. If the Altar Stone was given a clear dignified setting, then people would naturally gravitate towards it becoming an object of note, not an icon, but a symbol of light as originally intended.

As it is broken into two pieces, how could the Altar Stone be re-erected? The total length of the stone is estimated to be about four metres with the longest upper section of the stone measuring approximately two and half metres. So, in theory there is enough stone available to stand upright again with the remaining length resting in the ground as a supporting foundation. How though, would the remaining broken section be utilised? Could this be reconnected with its other piece or would a new replacement stone have to be brought in altogether? Whilst any of these options might be possible in the future, reaching agreement on the best solution would be a real problem.

The other more practical option would be to leave the stone remaining flat in the ground and quite simply move the stones sitting on top of it to one side. This is the option to which the archaeological profession and the custodians of Stonehenge are most likely to give further consideration. In order to look at how we might interact with a horizontal stone, we need to look at some other examples.

Other sacred stones of a similar nature

Stonehenge is not the only site where sacred stones are laid horizontal. The site of the Buddha's enlightenment, at Bodh Gaya in India, is marked by a sandstone slab known as the 'Diamond Throne' and is often decorated with offerings. Another example would be 'The Anointing Stone' of the Church of the Holy Sepulchre in Jerusalem. Here in the main entrance of the building a long flat stone is touched, kissed and anointed by pilgrims.

The Solstice Stone at Chartres Cathedral in France also has some similarities. Here, the light of the midsummer sun shines through a specially created hole in one of the stained glass windows and illuminates the stone set into the floor of Cathedral. Whilst this stone is generally not blessed like the Anointing Stone, people still come to look and wonder. Interestingly, the incorporation of the Solstice Stone points to the site's pre-Christian past. The location of the Cathedral was once reputed to be a place of ancient Druid worship and perhaps the intention of the builders was to incorporate any ancient earth energy lines into the more modern church structure above.

Reasons for change

There are some good practical reasons for moving the fallen stones of the Great Trilithon. At summer solstice the stones are stood, sat and even clambered upon. Over the years the Altar Stone has developed a clearly marked hollow from the feet of many visitors. Whilst this now only occurs at the major access times, the stone is still scuffed by footwear in an unconsidered and inappropriate manner. One potential solution to this problem would be to move the fallen stones of the Great Trilithon and create better definition within the inner space. Such a change could be to everyone's benefit.

The process of restoration and change at a holy site, however, can be fraught with disagreement and tensions no matter where it is in the world. Many years of negotiation had to take place between the various Christian dominations located within the Church of the Holy Sepulchre before restoration of the main dome could be completed in 1997. Further arguments about creating another doorway within the outer walls of the church have also been fraught with difficulty. The main entrance is the only way in and out and this is clearly not enough to satisfy health and safety requirements when large crowds gather. Pilgrims have been crushed in the past and if the same were to happen at Stonehenge access could well be restricted.

Revealing the Altar Stone

Revealing the two sections of the Altar Stone would open up the central area of Stonehenge to a whole new audience. Clear and attainable guidelines could then be agreed about how the solstice revellers and spiritual seekers could interact with the temple's inner heart. When the gates open on solstice eve, this space soon fills up with people jostling for the best view of the drumming. The issue of overcrowding will have to be taken into consideration sooner or later, as the present situation is unsustainable.

Crowds of people standing on top of the fallen stones of the Great Trilithon during the summer solstice celebrations 2006
Photograph by David Slater

With the stones moved, the inner heart could have its own entry and access points marked out with discreet handheld ropes or wooden barriers. This could even be done on a trial basis during the build up to sunset. The main body of the central circle would still be free for the impromptu summer solstice drummers and those wanting to come to the spiritual heart of the temple would be able to do so unimpeded. All these changes would turn the centre of Stonehenge into a more user-friendly space. Those out to party and those seeking a more contemplative experience could do so together.

The process of presenting new ideas is a major challenge for all those concerned with Stonehenge and the aim here is to stimulate meaningful debate about Stonehenge's future role. The journalist Simon Jenkins noted in the *Guardian* that: 'Stonehenge is a place of pagan worship and as such should be handed to those for whom it means something, the druids and astronomical clock watchers. They should be given a lottery grant and told to put the stones back in working order.'[35]

I believe that a genuine plan needs to be put forward.

Landscape architecture

Modern landscape architects often assess pedestrian movement and behaviour in order to design public spaces that work for the good of all. The work of the Danish landscape specialist Jan Gehl has been highly influential, as are so called 'space syntax' studies of how people interact with public space. The basic premise is that people want to feel safe and included by the provision of high quality public spaces incorporating well-designed seating arrangements, landscaping and other features for performance and social interaction. It is a natural instinct to want to go somewhere, 'to see what is going on' and 'watch the world go by'. Taking an evening stroll or promenade is a natural thing to do and is a feature of many a festival. Aside from the many theories, Stonehenge and its surrounding landscape are, in part, an early piece of landscape design. Redesigning such spaces as the centre of Stonehenge to meet modern needs can really improve the visitor experience of those using the site today.

Trafalgar Square in London would be a good example of how a modern civic space has been transformed through well considered design. The northern side of the square was pedestrianised and a new broad flight of steps, disabled access lifts, a café and toilet facilities were created. This process of renewal did take several years of negotiation to reach agreement with London Hackney cab drivers amongst others, who were fearful of losing the road space and any subsequent business through pedestrianisation. Completion of the revamp in 2003 breathed new life into the square and the changes have been a success.

Like Trafalgar Square, the centre of Stonehenge has now become a public space or theatre set which reflects back to us a picture of ourselves. There is room for a party at solstice, but there needs to be room for a socially inclusive atmosphere where everyone is made to feel welcome. Stonehenge has many functions and provides a platform for both public and private times of access. These can incorporate a whole range of activities from baby blessings and initiations to hand-fastings and services of remembrance. By allowing change to happen people will be able to find a new and more positive path within the temple's inner heart and this will solve many of the issues of overcrowding. The main elements of change are:

1. Only three stones to be moved, stone 156 – the Great Trilithon's lintel – and the two sections of the fallen pillar numbered 55 a and b. This will improve the clarity of the central area around the Altar Stone, which would remain horizontal in the ground. Following further consultation, further change could happen at a later date. This could include the option of whether to re-erect the Altar Stone and the fallen bluestone (stone 67), which lies nearby.

2. Stone 55a would be re-erected. This stone has a large bulbous base and would be able to stand on its own weight without the need of a concrete socket or other support. This simple move would be a gesture to the re-erection lobby and allow the setting sun at midwinter to find a clear, albeit tighter, setting space between the re-erected stone and existing standing pillar (stone 56) of the Great Trilithon.

3. 55b and 156 would be placed outside the main area. Here they would be placed in such a way to look as if they have fallen naturally in an outwards direction.

4. Everything else remains the same, including the main body of Stonehenge being cordoned off to the general public during normal public opening times throughout the rest of the year.

Stonehenge today, with the fallen stones of the Great Trilithon blocking the central area

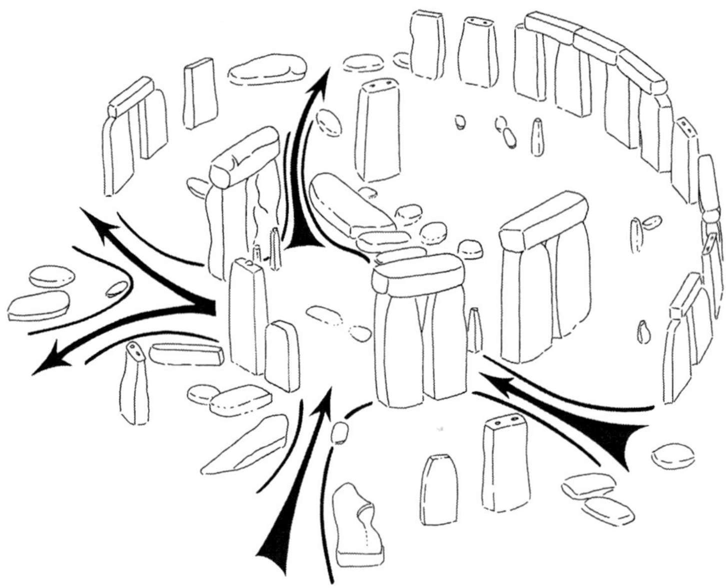

Proposed re-erection of one stone and movement of two other fallen stones to allow better access and definition within the centre area

In this photograph, I have lined up the outer stone (no. 16) with the Great Trilithon's standing pillar (stone 56) in order to give an impression of how the re-erected stone 55a may look. Note the Great Trilithon's fallen pillar and lintel in the foreground

The process of further investigation

There is a ground swell of archaeological opinion that would like to reinvestigate Stonehenge using modern scientific techniques. In 2005 David Miles, chief archaeology adviser to English Heritage, stated: 'It is over 50 years since substantial excavations have taken place at Stonehenge and more than two decades since the small excavations. This research gap needs to be rectified and, crucially, science can now reveal rich details. There is no site like this anywhere else in the world and we badly need to improve our understanding of it. This is not a call for an autopsy of the place. We are not going to make a mess. It will be more sensitive: more like targeted brain surgery.'[36]

A start was made to this process in the spring of 2008, when Professors Tim Darvill of Bournemouth University and Geoff

Wainwright, President of the Society of Antiquaries, were allowed to investigate the site and use the latest radio carbon dating techniques on excavated organic matter. They also wanted to give credence to their theory about Stonehenge being the 'Lourdes of the Bronze Age', whereby people came to access the healing properties of the mysterious bluestones. The bluestones were first identified as coming from a specific area of the Welsh Preseli Mountains in the 1920s. The professors spent a great deal of time studying this area which is known as Carn Menyn crags.

The professors were interested in the various natural springs which emerge from the base of the crags. They subsequently developed a theory of how clear spring water passing over crystalline rock may relate to healing. It is alleged that water can hold 'memory' as in the work of the Japanese researcher Masaru Emoto from the early 2000s. Emoto developed a technique whereby frozen water crystals can be photographed at high magnitude. He was then able to observe how the frozen crystalline structures were apparently affected by human thoughts, words and intentions. Other factors such as where the sample water originated also had a bearing on the results. Darvill and Wainwright's research resembled some of Emoto's ideas and linked folklore traditions of the stones being washed and the water used in baths for healing right up until early Victorian times. The excavation also revealed a lot of bluestone chippings which were possibly used as amulets or lucky charms in ancient times. A chipped piece of Stonehenge could have been a highly prized item, for it was thought that the crystalline rock could transmute a memory of freshness when used during bathing.

After the results of the dig had been analysed, Darvill and Wainwright put forward a date of 2300 BCE as to when bluestones first arrived on site and construction began. This resulted in some debate on the subject of dating, with other researchers stating that radio carbon dating can only provide a general picture. Techniques involving soil analysis and examining isotopes in bone and teeth fragments can provide a better level of understanding when it comes to establishing exact dates, according to Professor Parker Pearson.

The premise of Parker Pearson's Riverside Project was to substantiate existing theories about Stonehenge being a monument to the dead. The results have led to a whole new understanding of Stonehenge within the wider context of its ceremonial landscape. Essentially, the project concluded that midwinter was the main focus of celebration. Following excavations at Durrington Walls, the project team went on to unearth a special avenue link connecting the settlement with the nearby River Avon. The axis of this Avenue also aligned with the winter solstice sunrise. This evidence then suggests that the ancients walked down to the river's edge, via this link, before following its course downstream until they reached the start of the main Stonehenge approach Avenue. Here the archaeologists found evidence of another stone circle dubbed 'Bluestonehenge'. The pilgrims would then have processed up the main Avenue until they reached Stonehenge itself. Any cremated remains would then have been buried in special pits, now known as the Aubrey Holes. The dramatic sight of the midwinter sun setting right into the heart of the monument on the longest night of the year would then have been observed. This could well have represented the departing souls passing over into the afterlife. Processing back to Durrington Walls, the pilgrims would probably have witnessed the winter solstice sunrise on the next day. This sequence of events could have seen the ancients linking the return of the light with the passage of the dead spirits transcending into new life.

Prof. Parker Pearson concluded the Riverside Project in late 2008 with a re-excavation of one of the cremation pits or Aubrey Holes last investigated by Prof. Richard Atkinson in the late 1950s. Some controversy surrounds this final phase of Parker Pearson's dig, as some of the cremated remains ended up in storage and were not returned to the excavated hole in question. Despite this issue, the visual appearance of the excavated areas had to be put back more or less as found afterwards.

The 'Hidden Landscapes' project led by Prof. Vince Gaffney of Birmingham University, in conjunction with other professionals from Vienna's Ludwig Boltzmann Institute for Archaeology, continues the more recent investigations into the Stonehenge site. Using the latest ground penetrating radar magnetometers, their remit was to investigate and map the entire landscape within its original context. Media interest was aroused during the early days of surveying when the potential outline of another circle henge was claimed to have been found, although without excavation this is yet to be proven. Like most other archaeological investigations, this project aimed to understand the past, rather than develop a case for future change.

Investigating the Great Trilithon, however, would be another matter because any findings might support its partial re-erection. It was this lack of clear dating evidence which probably stopped Prof. Atkinson and his team from re-erecting some of the Great Trilithon's fallen stones in the late 1950s. These stones were not re-erected during the restoration programmes of the twentieth century due to the policy of only raising stones which had a recorded date of when they fell. The earliest recorded collapse was in 1797 and prior to that the dates and order as to when various stones fell are unconfirmed.

Establishing why and when the Great Trilithon fell would be a useful exercise. The general theory is that it fell by its own means, landing on top of the Altar Stone, thus breaking it in two. Perhaps modern techniques could produce evidence of foul play by weakening of postholes or use of fire to break the structure and finally establish a date as to when the structure might have fallen? We are not to know the answer to any of these questions, except by further investigation.

Using a range of dating techniques, as noted above, a date could now be established as to when the stones fell. A management plan could then be drawn up for redefining the central area, once the way forward had been agreed. Contractors could move the stones with a modern hydraulic crane in little more than a day with the surrounding uprights being protected by a special casing. No stone would be lifted over the tops of any other stone still standing. In a similar way to the 2008 Darvill and Wainwright excavation, a television company could provide funding and produce a supporting programme showing the entire process. The BBC history programme *Timewatch* funded the 2008 excavation for example. The project proposal presented here need not be extortionately expensive, even when the initial planning, preparation, labour, crane hire and cost of the supporting archaeological dig are all taken into account.

Conclusion

The ancients constantly played around with the configuration of stone circles, adapting them over time, bringing in new stones, reshaping and reusing others and even taking broken ones away. There needs to be a realisation that every now and again minor changes do need to happen for Stonehenge to remain fully functional. No one wants to see any restoration work carried out by resurrecting fallen stones with the aid of concrete sockets and a complete reconstruction of the monument would also be inappropriate. The simple movement of a few stones would be a middle course focusing on a more 'gentle approach'[37] as noted by the archaeologist Julian Richards in his book *Stonehenge: A History in Photographs.*

Revealing the Altar Stone would be an open acknowledgement of the temple's power and Britain's ancient nature-worshipping past. This could potentially lead to an increase in the number of general visitors and those seeking a spiritual connection with the place. We need to allow ourselves access to this ancient spot, as a place where we can touch the earth and be aware of ourselves and our environment. The male and female aspects of Stonehenge need to be balanced again with the Altar Stone representing Mother Earth and the principle of the Goddess taking a central role within the proceedings of free access.

Effective crowd management procedures are already in place and, in reality, a more open and friendly summer solstice celebration would find its own level and traditions for the participants and all those concerned with the site's upkeep.

Chapter 7

Proposals for the future

Introduction

Whilst the winter solstice and equinox gatherings remain relatively small occasions, many of the issues surrounding the future of the summer solstice celebrations require further debate. In this final chapter I will outline the work of the Round Table (RT) public access committee and examine some of the arguments and counter arguments as to the best way forward. I present a number of new ideas and ask a series of rhetorical questions about how the current situation could potentially be improved. There are many issues involved with 'improving' the celebrations, and the way forward is not always as easy as it might seem. How to implement change can also be an emotive issue. However, I still feel that it is a worthwhile exercise to discuss what is involved and to generally inform people about what goes on behind the scenes. This final section of the book is therefore presented in the format of a discussion document with the aim of stimulating debate and seeding ideas for the future.

Universal ownership and the work of the Round Table

No one group or person really owns Stonehenge and the idea of universal ownership was one of the main ideas associated with the original festival-goers. It is the current users of Stonehenge, however, who must decide what they want from the place and how any future changes can be achieved. This process continues under the watchful eye of the Round Table. The RT is made up of representatives from various Druid and Pagan groups and other interested parties and individuals. They meet on a regular basis in nearby Salisbury with members of English Heritage, the

National Trust, Wiltshire County Council and the emergency services, amongst others. In 2007, the timing of MOA was brought forward and extended to include the preceding summer solstice sunset. This change has proven to be a big success and is testament to the work of the RT.

One interesting question facing the future is the relationship between having the summer solstice celebrations as a free, open and spontaneous event, compared to one which has some greater level of input in terms of what actually 'happens'. On one hand, English Heritage does not see it as their role to organise a structured programme of events. On the other hand, why would many in the Pagan community want them to do this anyway? This creates a sometimes difficult situation concerning who is responsible for making things happen. The celebrations, however, are here to stay and what goes on does need to be given continued consideration by the authorities and representatives of the participants in terms of planning. This of course is the purpose of the RT, but progress can be slow and frustrating, as consideration again needs to be given to a whole range of differing opinions, health and safety requirements, monetary concerns and other regulatory factors.

Much of the surrounding landscape around the stones for example is deemed too archaeologically sensitive for tented structures (such as marquees, yurts and tipis) to be pegged into the ground. The issue of how to provide shelter is affected by this ruling and represents one of many areas where compromises need to be found. The implementation of a matted 'gathering area' for acoustic music and other performers in 2007 met with success. Perhaps this could be developed in the future with the use of more mats, a low rise rostrum or even self-supporting structures, such as geodesic domes. These could then be fixed into place with weights, rather than being pinned down into the ground. Such open and accessible structures could also be used to house tea tents and cafés.

One possible location for such structures would be on the site of the closed A344 road junction with the A303 to the east of the stones. This would be far enough away from the main circle to not be a visual distraction. Fewer archaeological restrictions apply to the ground beneath the road's surface at this point, so tents, yurts and other structures could actually be pegged down without too much problem. The possibility of using some of the former A344 road space to locate a larger fire brazier could also be investigated, as long as it was deemed to be safe, appropriate and compliant with current health and safety regulations. In addition to the existing MOA braziers located to the west of the stones, people would appreciate being able to stand reasonably close to another source of heat.

Providing an alternative focus to the revelry

On the ground, the big issue facing the future of the summer celebrations is moving some of the focus of the event away from the overly crowded party in the middle of the circle. The development of a plan of action to take the celebrations in this direction could ultimately be in everyone's interest.

There is much that could be learnt from solstice celebrations elsewhere. An annual summer solstice celebration is now held in Times Square, New York, for example and whilst this celebration is essentially based around yoga, some of the attractions are worth noting. In previous years there have been acrobatic and fire show performances. Amateur astronomers have also been on hand to give advice about how the sun affects our planet. The Times Square Alliance, who organise 'Solstice in the Square', amongst other events, are a 'not for profit' organisation. Their remit is to promote business and tourism by coordinating events that will showcase diversity and enhance the public realm. By providing activities the Times Square Alliance are offering an example of how to engage with an audience in a participatory manner.

Spiral labyrinth design

Whilst a labyrinth is not part of 'Solstice in the Square' the principle could easily be applied to MOA with a spiral design marked out on a reusable mat. This would allow people to take part in any number of activities, as noted earlier. Another idea would be to establish a thermal imaging camera linked to a display screen. This could then pick out the rising or setting sun through any mist or cloud cover. The resulting images could also be broadcast online. Although this goes against the idea of semi-structuring part of the event, these ideas, however hypothetical, would work well at Stonehenge, as only so much can happen spontaneously.

Letting things develop organically

The counter argument to all this is that semi-structuring any part of MOA goes against the free-spirited ideals of the original festival. The solstice represents a free space 'where anything goes' and if you want to see something happen then 'do it yourself' and 'bring what you expect to find'. To expect others to provide an evening of entertainment and sideshows could be regarded as heresy by those seeking a return to the spontaneity and creativity of old festival. The argument here is that people should just be able to turn up and do what they want for a few days, without the hassle of anyone telling them what to do. Any further organisation of modern access would only be 'sanitising' an already 'sanitised event'. However, change can happen when individuals and other community minded benefactors take the lead. In 2010, a company called A&R Metal Crafts brought a 6.7 metre high metal sculpture to the celebrations. Entitled *The Ancestor*, the sculpture depicted a kneeling man with his arms wide open to greet the sun. A&R Metal Crafts, however, had to spend time negotiating with English Heritage before this could happen. They also had to make the sculpture, transport it to the site, manage it whilst it was there, remove it afterwards and self-fund the whole project.

Amplified music and more opportunities to dance

Providing more music and opportunities to dance is an essential part of this debate. Amplified music was one of the key components of the free festivals prior to 1985. No matter how clichéd images of the spoof rock band Spinal Tap, the free festival regulars Hawkwind and even Led Zeppelin (who used a Stonehenge-inspired stage backdrop on their 1977 US tour) are to Stonehenge, the demand for a 'mass rave' remains in defiance of whatever viewpoint any modern observer may take. People are still looking to find a communal experience via music, dancing and vocal expressions of joy. It could therefore be argued that another free festival with mobile sound systems is the 'natural state of being' and is exactly what would appear given half a chance.

The party vibe remains forever bubbling under the surface, so why not plan to 'officially' incorporate it into the proceedings instead of continually trying to repress it? Dancing can provide people with moments of collective togetherness. For some, partying is a more direct way to celebrate the solstice and a spiritual experience in its own right. People, after all, have danced under the stars since the dawn of time.

Celebrating the solstice can certainly be fun, but basic amenities such as drinking water, refuse collection, recycling, toilets, first-aid and an organisational action plan still need to be provided for it to be a safe and pleasant environment for all to enjoy. Whilst these issues are certainly addressed during MOA, it could be argued that the summer celebration lacks the spark of an amplified music festival. Apart from the addition of the successful gathering area, where people can watch acoustic performances at their own pace, much of the musical focus still tends to be based around the drumming in the centre of the circle and the car stereos blaring out up in the solstice car park. This can sometimes be intimidating and even bewildering for those seeking an accessible party and place to dance. The authors of the book *Blighty* describe this aspect of the solstice as follows: 'We'd love to say we stayed up all night, dancing'[38] but, as they later point out, in reality, they didn't. At its worst the celebration can represent an awkward student house party with little or no atmosphere. Is it no wonder then, that many casual visitors can see the whole celebratory experience as being a little odd, as the revellers try to make the best out of a curtailed and restrictive situation? This too can lead to a point of conflict between those seeking a more contemplative spiritual experience and those out to party regardless of what else goes on around them. It is a sad fact that because of the overbearing crowd many choose to stay away altogether. The good news however, is that the popularity of the solstice continues to grow and the longest day of light is now celebrated at a range of other locations and sacred sites. Avebury is probably the best known of these, along with smaller celebrations at Glastonbury Tor, Castlerigg Stone Circle in Cumbria and the Rollright Stones amongst others.

Smaller summer solstice celebrations are increasingly held at other places apart from Stonehenge, like this one at the Rollright Stones on the Oxfordshire and Warwickshire border. This photograph shows the gathered crowd watching the sunrise by the King Stone in 2011
Photograph by Julie Robins

Inclusion and exclusion

Stonehenge has probably struggled with issues of inclusion and exclusion ever since it was first created. It is highly likely that the original ceremonies were the preserve of the privileged few allowed into the centre of the circle. Those left standing outside were probably not in a position to determine much of what was going on, let alone be involved in a practical way. This situation still carries on today with the crowds packed into the central area. On the outside many solstice visitors can easily find long periods of inactivity with a substantial number of people looking for something to do. This can only exacerbate the existing problems of drunkenness. How the current situation can be improved is one of the most difficult questions facing the future of the celebrations. One solution, as noted earlier, would be to create a number of different 'happenings' around the edge of the circle. People could then find things to do at their own pace. Yet this is no easy thing to even say, let alone put into practice. Those seeking a return to the days of the free festival for example, would state that it provided many of the extra activities so lacking during MOA.

Although the former free festival was more than a party, over the years partying has remained central to the solstice experience. What represents 'spirituality' can also be a difficult thing to define, as partying can also be 'spiritual' especially when combined with ecstatic dance for example. The authors of *Sacred Sites and Contested Rites / Rights* refer to this as: 'Sacred Partying'[39] and point out that it is just as valid as anything else.

Perhaps, in the longer term, an agreed form of 'amplified music' could be allowed back at a location near the stones? The celebrations really do need more music and opportunities to dance. Yet this remains a highly contentious issue, because of the spectre of it resembling the old festival in the eyes of the authorities. On a practical level, what type of music would be played, where would it be staged and how would it be organised? The authorities would also be concerned that a legitimised 'amplified' party would only encourage more people to attend.

Having said all that, a small number of organised drumming troupes could easily play a range of African, Arabic, Bhangra and Samba type rhythms. A calmer vibration would then take place among the stones, as the wandering revellers would then have somewhere to focus their attention. Funding, however, is very limited, if not totally non-existent, for the development of the celebrations. Although, it would be interesting to examine what effect the provision of more music might have on reducing the security bill. The King's Drummers, for example, have not appeared since 2008 and the number of arrests, mainly for public order offences, has grown slightly since then. This raises the legitimate question of whether some of the money spent on security would be better spent on providing music to keep people occupied.

The King's Drummers parade

Many of the early celebrations did feature a parade consisting of torchbearers, drummers and dancers in bright costume. This was put together by the Anthropology lecturers Lionel Sims and Chris Knight of the University of East London, along with a number of their students and the Barking Bateria samba band. During MOA they came under the title of the King's Drummers as tribute to the success of King Arthur Pendragon's long-running campaign for access prior to 2000.

In the end, the whole thing ultimately became a victim of its own success. The original route which formerly went all the way around the stones was cut back to a simple line running from the old visitor centre to just beyond the Heel Stone. The intention of the parade was to provide a focal point for the darkest part of the night, but due to the large numbers of people wanting to see what was going on, concerns were raised about health and safety. Security guards and a moveable rope barrier were provided, but because of ongoing safety, financial and other reasons the drummers no longer attend.

King's Drummers parade in 2007
Photograph by David Slater

Since the end of the parade there is not much else to see in terms of other visually eye-catching performances, as the former impromptu and unsupervised fire shows have also been suspended because of public safety. Even the welcome addition of the 'Sacred Soap Box', a chair-like platform for discussion, debate and performance, has had its fair share of fire risk assessments. Provided by a member of the Round Table public access committee, the soap box now stands well away from the stones for this reason.

Time for discussion at the 'Sacred Soapbox'

Replacing the King's Drummers with a co-ordinated show also has the downside of negating all those who do make the effort. The list of performers includes all those at the gathering area and other impromptu acts, such as the local Morris Dancers and even the drummers in the centre of the circle! The West Papuan dancers who appeared in 2009 and the Maori dawn choir from 2001 are just some of those who have made a welcome contribution over the years.

Whilst there are many plus points to the rule on non-amplification, one of the downsides is that many of the performances in the gathering area can be difficult to hear. At festivals, especially ones with a green ethos, amplification can be provided with the aid of solar panels, small wind turbines and even fixed-rack bicycles on which people have to keep pedalling in order to keep the music going! This is the sort of compromise which could provide power and pave the way forward. The creation of a sustainable dance zone away from the stones would help to spread people out over a wider area.

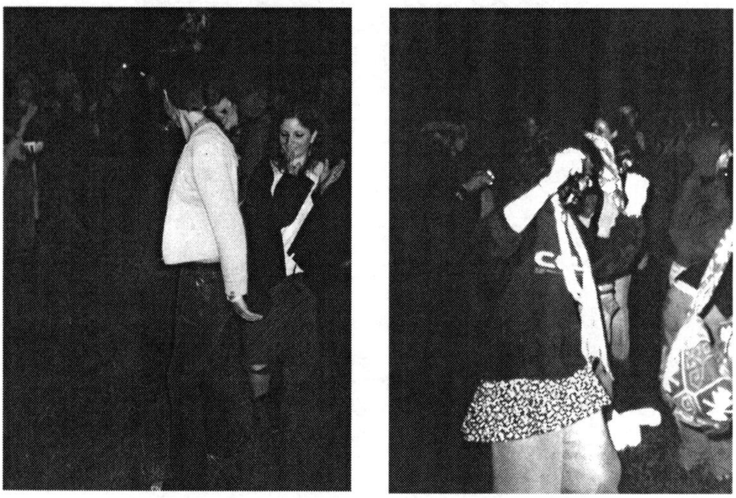

Some dancing does occur at Stonehenge usually in conjunction with the drumming, but more needs to be done to encourage dancing on a larger and more inclusive scale

Extending the solstice and creating more time for families

How appropriate it is to take a child to experience the hustle and bustle of the all-night party is obviously down to the parents and guardians concerned. But, having taken my then eighteen-month-old daughter to the celebrations in 2003, I later came to question whether this was a good idea. By focusing your visit down to either a few hours before sunset or around the sunrise you would still get a flavour of the event and have time to catch some sleep.

Whilst the main thrust of solstice access is based around the night and following dawn, some would like to see MOA spread out over a much longer period of time. Extending MOA up until twelve noon on the 21st June has been suggested. Here the sun reaches its highest position in the sky on the longest day. This midday moment is sometimes known as the 'eye of the sun' and is seen as having great symbolism. However, the main problem with extending access into the day of the 21st is how to combine fee-paying tourists with a group of revellers wanting to stay on and party. Having access during the night solves this problem, but daytime access would require a completely different set-up and is not something the authorities are in a hurry to even consider. Access on the evening of the celebrations however, has been getting earlier. In 2005 the stones opened at 22:00 but by 2009 this had been brought forward in stages to 19:00 hours. The opening time could possibly be brought forward again, once the new visitor centre opens and the A344 is finally grassed over. Extra time in the early evening would then increase the options for families and those seeking a more reflective period at the stones.

The circle of cooperation

Despite all the varying views on how to improve matters, debate is still ongoing about these and many other issues. The result of this is an ever-changing and developing MOA with the Round Table, a number of highly motivated groups and individuals playing a key role in steering the way forward. To this effect, a 'Vision Workshop' was organised by English Heritage and Round Table members during the spring of 2008. This brought together a whole range of people connected with the celebrations, many of whom had never met before. The main aim of the workshop was to look at how the celebrations might be developed in the future. One of the ideas mooted was the introduction of an eisteddfod, which is a festival of music, storytelling and poetry, along with promoting an expanded solstice celebration in conjunction with the local community. A start to this process was made on 1st May 2008 when a short period of ceremonial access was granted around midday for a prearranged group of Pagans to celebrate Beltane. May Day, or Beltane, marks the start of summer and this special point of access saw Maypole dancing and a short ceremony take place alongside normal daily visitors.

The summer solstice celebrations on the other hand, are at a turning point and could potentially become much bigger than at present. If attendance grows well beyond the 2009 high of 36,500, the solstice would then go up a bracket in the nation's consciousness. Greater coverage by the media would no doubt follow if the gathering attracted a much larger crowd of, say, 100,000 people. The celebrations would then be a lot more difficult to ignore. That is why the visioning process is the right way forward, as people need to picture how the future could look and how it will work in practice. The development of the celebrations is also part of the ongoing process whereby Paganism, with all its differing interpretations, is becoming more accepted by wider society. However, there is some speculation that most people who attend MOA are tourists, locals and revellers rather than actual Pagans who follow a distinctive path all year round.

Any proposals for change without a cross consensus of support are unlikely to be taken seriously by the authorities. The presentation of new ideas has to be done step by step with all the correct documentation and planning in place before anything happens. This means that progress can equally be as slow as it can be rewarding for those involved and, with regards to reintroducing the festival, a few voices of dissent still echo in the background. As well as the many achievements, there have been many arguments and disagreements along the path to change. Sadly, disillusionment, anger and even apathy have also had a part to play in this ongoing process.

But, things have changed and continue to change and people are now more willing to work together. In this respect the celebrations offer a vision of the future with many different groups of people coming together in the spirit of cooperation. It is now recognised that the solstice celebrations are a good thing and are there to be cherished. The meaning of the event is also recognised as representing different things to different people. I too, as the author of this book, accept that there are many other views in addition to the ones written on these pages. The stones it seems are a construct of the mind and all the possibilities which lay within it. The celebrations need more space to develop. Funding, however, remains the key to much of the above, as do the organisational structures in regards to making things happen.

A344 road closure and the new visitor centre

Opening up the landscape following the closure of the A344 road and construction of the new visitor centre will also help facilitate change. Closing the road will see the monument field extended. At the time of writing, English Heritage and the National Trust are in the process of agreeing how this will happen. Once the area has been opened up it will make it easier for people to spread out over a wider area running down from the Heel Stone. Druid orders will also have the option of processing up the Avenue to the stones as originally intended.

Further improvements to the A303

In the future I envisage, in part, more of a loosely defined A303 road working its way across the landscape. 'Shared Space' roads are a fairly new concept in the UK and early examples in Brighton, Ashford and at Seven Dials in London prove what is possible. A shared space road is where the existing road boundaries are removed and motor vehicles and other road users share some of the same space. The idea behind these schemes is that drivers then naturally slow down when faced with an unmarked road and a multitude of other users. However, there has been some criticism of such projects, especially from disabled groups and more recent schemes, such as the Exhibition Road project in London, do include a corridor for regular traffic.

At Stonehenge, any new project could involve creating a short section of 'natural-looking' A303 road running past the stones with a clearly marked vehicular corridor based around the existing single carriageway. This could be created by using green coloured 'low noise' asphalt and redesigning the boundary fences so that the roadway is still clearly defined, but less obtrusive. Any street clutter in the form of excessive signage would also be removed. The area in question would run between Stonehenge Bottom (the old junction with the A344) and the Bridleway running just to the west of the stones, a distance of about one kilometre. Traffic would be kept moving, but at a slower speed, so that drivers would realise they need to take extra care when passing through the World Heritage Site.

Some different thinking is needed as previous projects only aimed at building new roads and speeding up traffic. A reconfigured A303, however, could include a parallel footpath and a high quality 'Dutch standard' segregated cycleway. A crossing point could be created by constructing a discreet bridge over the A303 possibly linking the two lost sections of the Avenue back together. Inserting a subway through the existing embankment at Stonehenge Bottom would also be another idea. All this would form part of a wider pedestrian and cycle route linking the new visitor facilities with the nearby town of Amesbury. In time, these more cost-effective ideas will probably prove to be the only way forward for the A303, as large-scale road building is not acceptable in the vicinity of Stonehenge. The spirit of place will simply not allow it.

To be fair, English Heritage and the National Trust do have an ongoing management plan for the wider Stonehenge landscape and World Heritage Site. This involves returning much of the ploughed farming land to pasture and open grazing. There has also been some discussion regarding the removal of some non-indigenous coniferous planting and visible electric pylon lines from the horizon.

Conclusion

Theoretically, further change could happen if a private benefactor or other organisation was willing to spend money on developing MOA. But, as mentioned earlier, the whole peace and development process is really a balancing act between the various groups involved, and is it really English Heritage's responsibility to organise what could be seen as one of the largest Pagan events in Britain? The answer to this is both yes and no. Yes, because they manage the site and have to take health and safety into consideration, but also no as they are a public body there to promote heritage rather than Paganism. English Heritage finance and oversee MOA, but they do not direct what goes on. This is a very important point, as the celebrations are what they are. It is highly unlikely then, that English Heritage would take up many of the developmental ideas discussed in this section.

Whilst many of the changes suggested in this chapter would certainly help MOA move forward, people cannot necessarily be too reliant on things being that much different in the future. This does not mean, however, that new ideas cannot be put forward and suggestions made on how the gathering could potentially be improved. Ultimately, the future of Stonehenge lies within the hands of all those who have an interest in its upkeep and new ideas will come to pass in time if they have good reasoning and sound financial logic behind them. Stonehenge is not a problem, but an ongoing process of development and compromise.

That is why the celebrations have been allowed to develop from the ground up, rather than be imposed from the top down. In my view this has been the *right decision* with progress continuing through the existing channels. It all goes back to Stonehenge being all things to all people. People see things differently and the celebrations are a showcase of this diversity. It is a case of trying to cover as many different viewpoints as possible in order to seek a cross consensus of agreement. By allowing the whole experience to develop slowly, a firm base is being established. Open access remains an open ended question and the door is being deliberately left open, so that within that remit, attendees can make what they want out of the experience. Therefore to conclude, when attending the celebrations it is up to you to take responsibility for your own experience, as no one else is going to do it for you!

Appendices

Stonehenge Summer Solstice Table of Access

Year	Estimated & actual attendance figures Days of the week	Sunrise and Weather Report	Moon Phase	1974 to 1984 Free Festival 1978 Centre of Stonehenge closed off to the paying public. Full Moon at the Summer Solstice 1985 Battle of the Beanfield 1986 Stonehenge becomes a World Heritage Site 1997 Full Moon at summer solstice *Astronomical timing of solstice in brackets*
2000	6,000 Tuesday night / Wed morning	Rain	Waning moon	First year of Managed Open Access (MOA) with eight hours of access from 23:30 to 7:30
2001	14,500 Wed night / Thurs morning	Initial cloud cover	New Moon on the 21st	Access time extended to 11 hours, running from 22:00 to 9:00
2002	23,000 Thursday night / Friday morning	Raining	Waxing	Many leave early to watch England play Brazil in the World Cup (13.24 on 21st)
2003	30,000 Friday night / Saturday morning	Clear sunrise	Waning Moon	Modern solstice celebrations fall on a weekend for the first time, record crowd in attendance. 19:10 on 21st)

2004	21,000 Sunday night / Mon morning	Mist at sunrise	Waxing	King's Drummers parade a set of giant animal horns (00:57 on 21st). A Transit of Venus occurred earlier in the month on the 8th June
2005	23,000 Monday night / Tues morning	Clear sunrise with only a few wisps of cloud	Full Moon on the 22nd	King's Drummers parade a red effigy (06.46 on 21st)
2006	18,700 Tues night / Wed morning	Rain and cloud	Waning	King's Drummers parade a green man effigy. During the night heavy rain dampens proceedings. Lower attendance possibly due to the poor weather and people staying on at the nearby Somerset-based Sunrise Festival to watch England play Sweden in the World Cup (12:26 on 21st)
2007	24,093 Wed night / Thurs morning	Cloudy and overcast at dawn, brighter later	Waxing	Implementation of slightly extended and altered access times which included the sunset running from 20.30 to 08.00. This and the new gathering area prove to be a great success. Larger crowd due to the Glastonbury Festival starting the next day (18:06 on 21st)

2008	36,290 Friday night / Sat morning	Cloudy with some rain	Full Moon on the 18th	MOA was on a Friday night and there was a new record crowd of over 36,000 in attendance. Access brought forward to 20:00. The King's Drummers paraded a white-horned figure (23:59 on 20th)
2009	36,500 Saturday night / Sunday morning	Cloudy at sunrise brighter later	New Moon on 22nd	Celebrations fall on a Saturday night, new record crowd in attendance. Access to the stones brought forward to 19:00 giving a full 13 hours until 08:00 on the 21st. (05:45 on 21st)
2010	Around 20,000 Sunday night / Mon morning	Reasonably clear sunrise	Waxing	Astrological timing of the summer solstice at (11:28 on 21st). A 6.7 metre (20ft) high metal sculpture called *The Ancestor* was displayed as part of the celebrations
2011	18,000 Monday night / Tues morning	Rain and cloud	Waning	Heavy rain during the night and a mid-week solstice results in a smaller crowd than usual (17:16 on 21st)
2012	14,500 Wed night / Thurs morning	Heavy rain	Waxing	A Transit of Venus occurred earlier in the month on 6th June. *The Ancestor* sculpture returned to the stones. Astrological timing of summer solstice (23:09 on 20th)

2013	Thurs night / Friday morning		Full Moon on the 23rd	Astrological timing of the summer solstice (05:04 on 21st)
2014	Friday night / Sat morning		Waning	Celebrations due to coincide with a Friday night (10:51 on 21st)
2015	Saturday night / Sun morning		Waxing	Celebrations due to coincide with a Saturday night (16:38 on 21st)
2016			Full Moon on 20th Jun	Full Moon in connection with night of the solstice celebrations (22:34 on 20th)
2017			Waning	(04:24 on 21st)
2018			Waxing	
2019			Waning	
2020			New Moon on the 21st	

2021			Full Moon on the 24th	
2022			Waning	
2023			Waxing	
2024			Full Moon on the 22nd	
2025			Waning	
2026			Waxing	
2027			Waning Full Moon on the 19th	
2028			Waning New Moon on the 22nd	
2029			Waxing	

2030			Waning	
2035			Full Moon	Full Moon in connection with the celebrations
2054			Full Moon	Full Moon in connection with the celebrations
2061				Halley's comet next due in Britain 28th July 2061
2090				Total solar eclipse due on mainland UK on Saturday 23rd September coinciding with the time of the Autumn Equinox. Stonehenge will be right on the edge of the line of totality

Please note the information compiled in the Solstice Tables of Access is to the best of my knowledge correct and I accept no legal liability for any loss, damage or disappointment caused through its intended use. Subsequent years have been left blank for you to fill in your own record of events.

Winter Solstice Table of Access

Year	Attendance	Weather Report	Date of MOA Dawn Access Sunrise usually around 8.09am (Astronomical Timing in brackets below)	Winter Solstice Managed Open Access Notes
2000	Around 100			
2001	100 to 200?		21st Dec.	
2002	300 to 400		(22nd 01:14)	
2003	300 to 400		(22nd 07:04)	
2004	Around 600	Cloudy	Tuesday 21st Dec. (21st 12:42)	Clear sunset reported at the winter solstice
2005	1,500	Cloudy	Wednesday 21st Dec. (21st 18:35)	Attendance at the winter solstice more than doubled since 2004

2006	1,500	Cloudy	Friday 22nd Dec. (22nd 00:22)	Official winter solstice access on the 22nd. However, around 60 people turned up the day before thinking the solstice was on the more usual day. English Heritage allowed a short period of unofficial access on the 21st
2007	1,700	Sunrise just visible thru' the mist	Saturday 22nd Dec. (22nd 06:08)	Record crowd in attendance for the dawn gathering on the 22nd. Unfortunately there was one arrest right at the end of MOA
2008	1,900	Misty at first, sun visible later	Sunday 21st Dec. (21st 12:04)	Attendance grows yet again with a crowd of nearly 2,000 present
2009	Around 300 on Mon 21st and about 700 on Tuesday 22nd	Cloudy at dawn	MOA access on Tuesday 22nd (Mon 21st 17:47)	Clear sunset on Sunday 20th Dec. Although the exact timing for the 2009 winter solstice was on the 21st (17:47) this time fell after sunset, so the official period of MOA was on Tues 22nd
2010	Over 2000	Grey cloud	MOA access on Wednesday 22nd (21st 23:38)	Full Moon on the 21st December with lunar eclipse in the morning. Grey cloud and mist obscure visibility of both the moon and the sunset and sunrise. Record crowd in attendance despite the snowy conditions

2011	Over 1000 with a few hundred on the 21st	Sunrise visible after an initially cloudy start	MOA access on Thursday 22nd (22nd 05:30)	About 450 take part in a midwinter's eve lantern procession from Stonehenge to Amesbury. Official access on the 22nd December
2012			MOA access on Friday 21st (21st 11:11)	
2013			(21st 17:11)	
2014			(21st 23:03)	
2015			(22nd 04.48)	
2016			(21st 10:44)	
2017			(21st 16:28)	
2018				
2019				
2020				

The Wheel of the Year

Summer Solstice (*Longest Day*) usually around 21st June

Lammas (*First Harvest*) 1st August

Autumn Equinox (*Equal Night and Day)*
on or around 23rd September

Halloween (*Growing Dark*) 31st October

Winter Solstice (*Longest Night*)
usually falls on either the 21st or 22nd December

Candlemas (*Growing Light*) 2nd February

Spring Equinox (*Equal Day and Night*) on or around 21st March

May Day/Beltane (*Fertility*) 1st May

Please note, that midsummer's day actually falls three days after summer solstice (24th June) and the rebirth of the sun occurs some three days after the winter solstice. However, throughout this book I have interchanged the terms solstice and midsummer/winter and not used the Celtic terms such as Litha and Yule for reasons of convenience.

REFERENCES

1. WORTHINGTON, Andy, 2004, *Stonehenge Celebration and Subversion*, Alternative Albion, Loughborough, page 240
2. PENDRAGON, Arthur, 1998, 'Sacred Sites – A Paper Prepared for the Association of Sacred Landscapes', online at: http://www.warband.org.uk/sacred/sites.htm
3. PITTS, Mike, 2000, *Hengeworld*, Century Press, page 232
4. HARVEY, Graham & HARDMAN, Charlotte, 2001, *Pagan Pathways*, HarperCollins, Introduction Section, page XI
5. Loyal Arthurian Warband (LAW) Druids online at: http://www.warband.org.uk/page21.htm
6. WRIGHT ARTHEN, Walter, online at: www.earthspirit.com/fireheart/fhwkman.html
7. MORETON, Cole, 22nd June 2009, 'Everyone's a Pagan now', *Guardian* newspaper article, G2 Supplement, page 7
8. KINDRED, Glennie & GARNER, Lu, 2002, *Creating Ceremony*, self-published book by the authors, page 6
9. GRAVES, Tom, 1980, *Needles of Stone*, Granada Publishing, London, page 147
10. BBC News 9th January 2001, online at: http://news.bbc.co.uk/1/hi/world/south_asia/1108154.stm
11. LOWE, Steve & McARTHUR, Alan, 2008, *Blighty – The Quest for Britishness*, Sphere Books, London, page 70
12. STARHAWK, online at: www.reclaimingquarterly.org/83/rq-83-makingitreal.html
13. Ibid., STARHAWK, as 12
14. BRYANT, Giles, 'A Guide to Working at Sacred Sites' pamphlet extract and online at: www.worldhealingproject.com
15. Northern Antiquarian online at: http://megalithix.wordpress.com/2008/07/24/httpwp-mepi6d8-c/

16. Zen saying online at: www.onmarkproductions.co.uk/html/stone-water-basins.html
17. BUDDHAMIND, online at: www.buddhamind.info/leftside/lifestyl/circum.htm
18. TOLAND, John, online at: www.sacred-texts.com/mas/sof/sof23.htm
19. COLEMAN, Simon & ELSNER, John 1995, *Pilgrimage – Past and Present in World Religions*, British Museum Press, pages 32–33
20. ARTHEN, Andras Corban, 1984, Words to 'Air I am, Fire I am ...' online at: www.earthspirit.com and www.reclaimingquarterly.org
21. PURNA, Svami, 1998, *Yoga: A Practical Introduction*, Element Books, Shaftesbury, Dorset, page 61
22. REA, Shiva, online at: www.yogajournal.com/practice/2579
23. COOKE, Grace & Ivan, 1971, *The Light in Britain*, White Eagle Publishing Trust, page 54
24. CHIPPINDALE, Christopher, 2004, *Stonehenge Complete*, Thames & Hudson, London, page 6
25. English Heritage Terms and Conditions online at: www.english-heritage.org.uk/summersolstice
26. VARNER, Gary, *Menhirs, Dolmen and Circles of Stone: The Folklore and Magic of Sacred Stone*, Algora Publishing, page 19
27. GRAVES, Tom, 1980, *Needles of Stone*, Granada Publishing Ltd. St. Albans, Herts, page 51
28. MEADEN, Terence, 1999, *The Secrets of the Avebury Stones*, Frog Press Ltd. Berkeley, California, page 140
29. MEADEN, Terence, 1997, *Stonehenge – The Secret of the Solstice*, Souvenir Press, page 108
30. PARKER PEARSON, Mike, as referenced in an article by WIGNALL, Alice, Tuesday 3rd January 2006, online at: http://www.guardian.co.uk/education/2006/jan/03/workinprogress.highereducation
31. COOPER, Keith, 1976, online at: www.northlight-images.co.uk/picture.php?id+88&kid=0
32. HAWKINS, Gerald, 1977, *Stonehenge Decoded*, Fontana/Collins, pages 200–201

33. ATKINSON, Richard, 1979, *Stonehenge*, Pelican Books, Harmondsworth, Middlesex, pages 211 and 212
34. NICHOLS, Ross, Order of Bards, Ovates and Druids (OBOD) online at: http://www.druidry.org/obod/theorder/archive/rn-bookdruidry.htm
35. JENKINS, Simon, 27th January 2006, 'The Curse of Stonehenge will remain until it is handed back to the Druids', *Guardian* newspaper article online at: www.guardian.co.uk/artanddesign/2006/jan/27/heritage.society7, site accessed 8/5/2006
36. McKIE, Robin, 2005, 'Scientists Seek Fresh Chance to Dig up Stonehenge's Secrets', 24th July 2005, online at: http://www.guardian.co.uk/science/2005/jul/24/research.highereducation, site accessed 24/1/2006
37. RICHARDS, Julian, 2004, *Stonehenge: A History in Photographs,* English Heritage, page 27
38. LOWE, Steve & McARTHUR, Alan, 2008, *Blighty – The Quest for Britishness*, Sphere Books, London, page 70
39. BLANE, Jenny & WALLIS, Robert, 2007, *Sacred Sites, Contested Rites / Rights*, Centre for Human Rights', Sussex Academic Press, 'Sacred Partying', page 97

BIBLIOGRAPHY

ATKINSON, Richard, 1960, *Stonehenge*, Pelican Books

BALFOUR, Michael, 1983, *Stonehenge and its Mysteries*, Hutchinson

BENDER, Barbara, 1998, *Stonehenge – Making Space*, Berg Books

BENNETT, Paul, 2008, 'The Northern Antiquarian', online at: http://megalithix.wordpress.com/2008/07/24/httpwp-mepi6d8-c/

BLAIN, Jenny and WALLIS, Robert J, 2007, *Sacred Sites, Contested Rites / Rights*, Centre for Human Rights, Sussex Academic Press

BRYSON, Bill, 1996, *Notes from a Small Island*, Black Swan

BURL, Aubrey, 1983, *Prehistoric Astronomy and Ritual*, Shire Publications

CARR-GOMM, Philip, 1991, *The Elements of the Druid Tradition*, Element Books

CARR-GOMM, Philip, 2006, *What do Druids Believe*, Granta Publications, London

CHIPPINDALE, 2004, Christopher, *Stonehenge Complete*, Thames & Hudson

CONWAY, D.J., 2001, *Wicca: The Complete Craft*, The Crossing Press

COOKE, Grace & Ivan, 1971, *The Light in Britain*, White Eagle Publishing Trust

COPE, Julian, 1998, *The Modern Antiquarian*, Thorsons

DEVEREUX, Paul, 2002, *Stone Age Soundtracks: The Acoustic Archaeology of Ancient Sites*, Vega Publishing

EHRENREICH, Barbara, 2008, *Dancing in the Streets – A History of Collective Joy*, Granta Books

EMOTO, Masaru, 2005, *The True Power of Water*, Simon and Schuster

FIRSTOFF, George, 1992, *History of the Troubles* – Why we need Stonehenge' online at: http:www.greenleaf.demon.co.uk/wwns.htm

GEHL, Jan, 1987, *Life Between Buildings*, Van Nost. Reinhold Press

GRAVES, Tom, 1980, *Needles of Stone*, Granada Publishing

GRIFFYN, Sally, 2000, *Sacred Journeys, Stone Circles and Pagan Paths*, Kyle Cathie Ltd

HARRINGTON, Philip, 1997, *Eclipse! The What, Where, When, Why and How Guide to Watching Solar and Lunar Eclipses*, John Wiley & Sons, Inc.

HARVEY, Graham & HARDMAN, Charlotte, 2001, *Pagan Pathways*, Thorsons / HarperCollins

HAWKINS, Gerald, 1970, *Stonehenge Decoded*, Fontana William Collins

HEATH, Robin, 2000, 'Stonehenge – The Marriage of the Sun and Moon', online at: http://cura.free.fr/decem/06heath.html

HUTTON, Ronald, 1996, *Stations of the Sun*, Oxford University Press

JELLICOE, Geoffrey & Susan, 1995, *The Landscape of Man*, Thames & Hudson

KINDRED, Glennie & GARNER, Lu, 2002, *Creating Ceremony*, self-published by Glennie Kindred and Lu Garner

KUMAR, Satish, 'Pilgrim or Tourist', *Something Understood*, BBC Radio Four Programme first broadcast Sunday 14th March 2010, a Loftus production for Radio Four

LETCHER, Andy, 2006, *Shroom – A Cultural History of the Magic Mushroom*, Faber & Faber

LOWE, Steve & McARTHUR, Alan, 2008, *Blighty – The Quest for Britishness*, Sphere

MARTIN, Christina, 2000, *Holy Wells in the British Isles*, Wooden Books

McKAY, George, 2000, *Glastonbury – A Very English Fair*, Victor Gollancz Publishers, An Imprint of Orion Books

MEADEN, Terence, 1991, *The Goddess of the Stones*, Souvenir Press Ltd

MEADEN, Terence, 1997, *Stonehenge – Secret of the Solstice*, Souvenir Press

MERZ, Blanche, 1987, *Points of Cosmic Energy*, CW Daniel Company Ltd
MINTON, Anna, 2009, *Ground Control – Fear and happiness in the twenty-first century*, Penguin Books
MITCHELL, John 1986 Edition, *The New View over Atlantis*, Thames & Hudson
NICHOLS, Ross, 'Book of Druidry', Order of Bards, Ovates and Druids, online at: www.druidry.org
NORTH, John, 1996, *Stonehenge – Neolithic Man and the Cosmos*, HarperCollins
PALMER, Martin, *Sacred Nation*, BBC Radio Two programme first broadcast 13th February 2005
PAXMAN, Jeremy, 1998, *The English – A Portrait of a People*, Penguin Books
PEDERICK, Richard, 1998, 'Save our Sacred Sites', online at: www.bath.ac.uk/~prsrlp/kernunos/ksoss.htm
PENDRAGON, Arthur & STONE C.J., 2003, *The Trials of Arthur, The Life and Times of a Modern Day King*, Element Books
PENDRAGON, Arthur, 2012, 'Sacred Sites', online at: www.warband.org.uk/page26.htm
PITTS, Mike, 2000, *Hengeworld*, Century Press
POLLARD, Joshua & REYNOLDS, Andrew, 2002, *Avebury – Biography of a Landscape*, Tempus Publishing
PURNA, Svami, 1999, *Yoga: A Practical Introduction*, Element Books
RECLAIMING QUARTERLY, online at: www.reclaimingquarterly.org
RESTALL ORR, Emma, 2004, *Living Druidry*, Piatkus Books
RICHARDS, Julian, 2004, *Stonehenge: a History in Photographs*, English Heritage
SCOTT PECK, M., 1997, *In Search of Stones*, Simon & Schuster
SIMS, Lionel, *Stonehenge the True Story*, Channel Five television programme, first broadcast 5th Aug 2001
SOUDEN, David, 1997, *Stonehenge – Mysteries of the Stones and Landscape*, English Heritage
STARHAWK, 1979, *Spiral Dance*, Harper San Francisco
STARHAWK, 2004, *The Earth Path*, Harper San Francisco

SULLIVAN, Danny, 2000, *Leys – Secret Spirit Places in Ancient Britain*, Wooden Books

TIMES SQUARE ALLIANCE, online at: www.timessquarenyc.org/events/solstice-in-times-square/index.aspx

TOLBOT, Michael, 1991, *The Holographic Universe*, HarperCollins

TRUBSHAW, Bob, 2005, *Sacred Places, Prehistory and Popular Imagination*, Heart of Albion

VARNER, Gary R, 2004, Menhirs, Dolmen and Circles of Stone – The Folklore and Magic of Sacred Stone, Algora Publishing

WARBURTON, Amy, 'The Summer Solstice', *Green Parent* magazine article, June / July 2005

WHITEHOUSE, David, 2006, *The Sun – A Biography*, Wiley Books

WILLIAMS, Lynn, 2002, *Rituals for and Enchanted Life*, Rider Press

WILLIAMS, Sheridan, 1996, *UK Solar Eclipses*, Clock Tower Press

WORTHINGTON, Andy, 2004, *Stonehenge, Celebration and Subversion*, Alternative Albion

Lightning Source UK Ltd.
Milton Keynes UK
UKOW04f0645220414

230356UK00010B/178/P

9 780956 219084